Strategic Direction and Development of the School

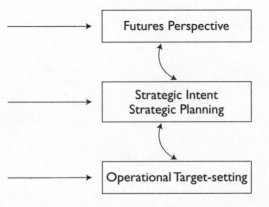

The thicker the plan the less it affects classroom practice

We cannot plan in schools for the new millennium by simply doing more of the same. As the educational environment becomes more complex and the demands on schools increase, the solution cannot be longer and more detailed school development plans. New demands and new times call for radical thinking. This book provides that thinking. It details a new approach to school planning through a framework which should help schools to meet the dynamic conditions of the Twenty-first Century while responding to current pressures and demands. This framework will allow schools to cope with complexity without overburdening them with more and more detailed planning matrices.

This book is designed for headteachers, deputy headteachers, governors and those participating in NPQH and masters programmes in educational leadership and management.

Brent Davies is Professor and Director of the International Educational Leadership Centre at the University of Lincolnshire and Humberside.

Linda Ellison is Principal Lecturer in Educational Leadership at Leeds Metropolitan University and editor of *Management in Education*.

Strategic Direction and Development of the School

Brent Davies and Linda Ellison

London and New York

First Published 1999
by Routledge
11 New Fetter Lane, London EC4P 4EE

Simultaneously published in the USA and Canada
by Routledge
29 West 35th Street, New York, NY 10001

Typeset in Palatino by
J&L Composition Ltd, Filey, North Yorkshire
Printed and bound in Great Britain by
Page Brothers (Norwich Ltd)

British Library Cataloguing in Publication Data
A catalogue record for this book is available from the British Library

Library of Congress Cataloging in Publication Data
Davies, Brent, 1949–
    Strategic direction and development of the school/Brent Davies
    and Linda Ellison.
    p. cm.
    Includes bibliographical references (p.) and index.
    1. School management and organisation – Great Britain.
    2. Educational planning – Great Britain. 3. Strategic planning –
    Great Britain. I. Ellison, Linda. II. Title.
    LB2900.5.D387   1998
    371.2′00941–dc21   98-7082
                                                              CIP

ISBN 0–415–18917–9

This book is dedicated to Rhiannon Brent Davies
for excellent 'A' level results and gaining a place at university

Contents

List of figures

List of tables

Foreword

This book is an essentially practical guide to school planning based on some radical thinking in times of rapid and continual educational change. Brent Davies and Linda Ellison, with contributions from senior staff in primary and secondary schools, have achieved their purpose of creating new knowledge of what is an appropriate and useful approach to planning for the year 2000 and beyond.

There are three particularly helpful threads running through the book.

The links are established between the long-term view of planning (futures thinking), medium-term issues (strategic intent and strategic planning) and the short-term need for operational target-setting.

There is a clear rationale behind this planning model and it is illustrated with a wealth of practical examples.

The importance of effective school leadership is stressed as a means of harnessing the range of options available to schools in a constantly changing world which offers many exciting opportunities but which also presents distractions from school improvement and raising standards of pupil achievement.

It should be essential reading for all those who care passionately about education. It encourages new approaches whilst at the same time providing strategies to secure continuous improvement in the quality of teaching and learning, pupil achievement and overall standards in schools. It is about riding the waves of change successfully while having an eye around the corners of the future.

Howard Green

Previously headteacher of two secondary schools ~ now working on the national programmes for the development of school leadership

Acknowledgements

We would like to thank the following for working with us and developing our ideas:

Mike Ainsley, Frederick Gent School, Derbyshire
Carol Barton-Jones, Birley Secondary School, Sheffield
Mike Billingham, The London Leadership Centre
David Black, Alsager Comprehensive School, Cheshire
David Bowes, St. James C. of E. School, Bolton
Stephen Box, Homer Green Upper School, High Wycombe
Ingrid Bradbury, Arbour Vale School, Berkshire
Michael Brearly, King Henry VIII School, Monmouth
Jane Cambrook, St John the Baptist (CE) Primary School, Hampshire
Gareth Davies, Knowles Hill School, Devon
John Forshaw, Rhyddings School, Lancashire
Kenny Frederick, George Green's School, London
Jane Fulford, Winton Primary School, London
Roger Glegham, Pearson Primary School, Hull
Ian Goodall, Yately School, Hampshire
Barry Gransden, Cromer High School, Norfolk
Peter Hargrave, Broughton Junior School, North Lincolnshire
Seonaid Hamilton, John Stainer Primary School, London
David Hornbeck, Philadelphia
Bob Johnson, Don Valley High School, Doncaster
Judith Lund, Healey Primary School, Rochdale
Marilyn Kinnon, London
Alan Marchant, Lincoln School of Management
Ian Mather, Southfield Community College, London
John McKinlay, St Joseph's RC Primary School, London
Christine Metcalf, Kent College, Kent
Barry Niedergang, Swansea
Annetta Padmore, Heber Primary School, London
Gary Saul-Paterson, Barrow Hill Junior School, London

Barbara Peck, The City of Lincoln Community College, Lincoln
Carol Penney, Baytree School, Somerset
Vicki Phillips, Children First, Philadelphia, USA
Keith Powell, Shepherd's Spring Junior School, Andover
Martin Rawson, The Castle Hills GM School, Gainsborough
Hugh Robinson, Minster College, Kent
Sue Robinson, Harrow Gate Primary School, Stockton-on-Tees
Carolyn Sabin-Young, Sir Fredrick Osborn School, Hertfordshire
Melanie Saunders, The Philip Morant School, Colchester
Jane Sutcliffe, Rosehill Infant School, Stockton-on-Tees
Mike Taylor, Greenwood Dale GM Technology School, Nottinghamshire
Christine Weaving, Breakspear Infant School, Middlesex
Jan Woodhead, Abbeydale Grange School, Sheffield
The staff of The Philip Morant School, Colchester, Essex
The staff of St. Thomas the Apostle School, London

Chapter 1

Introduction

The thicker the plan the less it affects classroom practice! We cannot plan in schools for the new millennium by simply doing more of the same. As the educational environment becomes more complex and the demands on schools increase, the solution cannot be longer and more detailed school development plans. New demands and new times call for radical new thinking. This book provides that thinking. It details a new approach through a framework which should help schools to meet the dynamic conditions of the twenty-first century while responding to current pressures and demands. This framework will allow schools to cope with complexity without overburdening them with more and more detailed planning matrices.

Planning has become a central aspect of leadership and management in schools over the last ten years. To reinforce the centrality of planning, we have now seen the development of the National Standards for Headteachers in which the first of the key areas for headship is 'Strategic Direction and Development of the School'. The inspection process has resulted in reports that encourage schools to extend short-term plans into a strategic framework and to produce three- or five-year costed plans. Planning is seen as desirable, necessary and (often, but mistakenly!) as a solution for poor management practice. Much of this planning work has, however, been linear and incremental in nature and no longer meets the needs of schools.

The last ten years have seen a period of intense activity to construct school development plans, spurred on by the requirements of the DES/DFEE and the Office for Standards in Education. A significant amount of the literature and resources on school planning was published in the early 1990s to support the process. Our first book on school development planning (Davies and Ellison 1992) was based on work that we had undertaken with several hundred headteachers who were responding to the challenge of designing appropriate planning structures and processes to meet the demands of self-management. The early 1990s saw a number of other publications in the field, with *Planning for School*

Development (DES 1989) being supported by *Development Planning: A Practical Guide* (DES 1991) and writers such as Hargreaves and Hopkins (1991), Skelton *et al.* (1991), West and Ainscow (1991) and Puffitt *et al.* (1992) picking up the theme. Later work by MacGilchrist *et al.* (1995) and Broadhead *et al.* (1996) has deepened our understanding of the process of development planning in schools.

There have been responses to our earlier work from a great many schools and from other authors. We have been heartened and encouraged by the large number of positive communications that we have received about how useful practitioners found the first book and how they have taken and adapted our ideas to form workable planning approaches. In terms of our critics, we offer no response to the criticisms made by Gunter (1997) except to draw the reader's attention to reviews of her work.[1] MacGilchrist *et al.* (1995) criticised the lack of a research base in our earlier work. This criticism we take head on. While we see that there is value in the work of MacGilchrist and her colleagues who research into nine primary schools and try to abstract universal truths about school planning, the timing of this work displays the limited value of some research for practitioners in the real world of education. Advice in 1995 about school planning would have been of little use to the practitioner struggling to establish coherent planning models in 1992!

In this new book we do not intend to deconstruct the plans of a few atypical schools in order to understand how a 1992 model may work in the year 2000. Rather, once again, we aim to take a reengineering approach. We draw on the experience of the many headteachers and schools with whom it has been our privilege to work during the last three years, in order to try to create the new knowledge of what is an appropriate and useful approach for school planning for the year 2000 and beyond. This book is, by its nature, forward-looking and proactive in its approach; it is research about practice and ideas and not an historical account of practices that have long been superseded. We consider that, as schools have taken over much of the role previously carried out by the LEA, they need to maximise their potential for action as self-managing institutions by fundamentally rethinking their planning processes. The reform and restructuring of education in the ten years between 1988 and 1998 can be seen as the 'first wave' of reform. It was largely focused on structural changes: national curriculum and testing frameworks; decentralised school structures; external inspection systems. In the choice of change strategy, many in education would suggest that change was done *to* schools rather than done *with* schools, leading to the conclusion that schools were often 'done in'! We now see a 'second wave' of reform which is not a series of structural initiatives sent down *to* schools but a series of reforming and reengineering improvements *within* schools with a focus on learning processes. While the initial period of delegation of financial and other responsibilities resulted in the setting up of systems which focused on efficient management, as schools' experience and expertise has grown, more creative strategies have been employed. Just as schools have moved on in their overall leadership and management approaches as a feature of this 'second wave,' so the emphasis and the nature of planning needs to change radically in schools. Our research, reported in Chapter 2, suggests that, while schools are successful in short-term operational planning, the longer-term 'strategic' or 'futures' perspectives still need developing.

Much confusion has arisen with terms such as strategic planning so that, for example, the National Audit Office (1994: 41) talks about the 'annual strategic planning cycle' which could, more correctly, be considered to be an operational plan. The tendency in the educational literature has been to tack 'strategy' onto development planning (see Giles 1997) without much consideration of the significant difference between the nature of strategy and traditional development planning. Furthermore, just as development planning was achieving acceptance in UK schools, Mintzberg (1994) was publishing his book *The Rise and Fall of Strategic Planning* which suggested that 'strategic planning' might be considered an oxymoron and that, at its worst, it prevented strategic thinking.

The purpose of this book is to remedy these shortcomings by putting forward a new model of planning for schools which suggests that they should operate three interactive planning activities/strands. Firstly, the misnamed 'development planning' should be renamed 'operational target-setting'. It is misnamed because 90 per cent plus of the budget or activity in the school is spent on maintaining or continuing current activities and less than 10 per cent on new ones. Consequently, this activity is better articulated as operational planning because the schools need to build 'operational targets', especially as a result of government pressure and legislation.

The second activity concerns strategy. We consider in depth the limits of strategic planning for anything other than the most predictable activities and develop a concept called strategic intent. Strategic intent is concerned with focusing on building, over the medium-term, capability in key areas of the school's activity without the paranoia of trying to produce detailed plans that are rapidly overcome in a turbulent environment. Thus, we see the building of strategic intent alongside traditional strategic planning as the second strand of an effective planning process. Thirdly, schools need to be aware of longer-term, and often global, trends that will impact on the fundamental nature of learning and schools as we know them. To understand these factors, schools need to use futures thinking in order to build a 'futures perspective' in the school. This new model of planning can be seen in the following diagram:

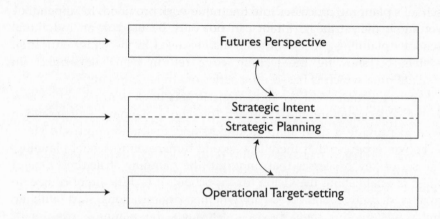

Figure 1.1 The reconceptualised model of school planning.

The model should not be interpreted as a hierarchical one but one in which the school is operating on the three planning activities or strands concurrently (four if strategy is split into the two parts). While ideas flow between the strands, it is important that the leader of the school and the staff in general are operating on all the strands. These are not discrete and linear processes.

In this book then, we seek to establish new ways of thinking and operationalising school planning. The book is aimed at all those in leadership and management positions in schools who are reviewing and re-examining their planning processes. As well as headteachers and governors it is aimed at deputy headteachers in the primary and secondary sectors, especially those working towards the National Professional Qualification for Headship (NPQH) or Masters qualifications, where we believe that it will provide key reading and ideas.

The book is organised so that we provide an overview of the new model by means of an executive summary of our work and the development of our thinking in Chapter 2. In Chapters 3 to 7 we build up in detail each of the component parts of the new model. Thus futures thinking, building strategic intent and creating strategic plans become the central thrust of the book alongside the transformation of traditional development plans into operational target-setting plans. We illustrate this latter process by school case examples from Howard Kennedy, Sue Cowans and David Jones (in Chapters 8 and 9). They describe the practical work that is being undertaken in a primary and a secondary school respectively on target-setting.

In Chapter 10 we outline the new model in its entirety. To test out the applicability of this model we utilise the expertise of a leading headteacher, Rob Gwynne, to give an account of how he has translated his school's planning processes into the framework provided. In Appendix 1 we show that strategic intent can not only be used in an individual school's planning process but can also be used in the wider education system by showing the leading edge reform being undertaken in Philadelphia which is based on a series of strategic intents.

We realise that what we have done in this book is to provide a new framework, structure and approach for school planning. Our intention was to provide a clear map to understand this new approach. However, we recognise that there is a second dimension to school planning: the set of key processes that underpin the planning structures. One of these is establishing the vision for the school. It is difficult, of course, to give a definitive answer as to whether organisations start with an initial vision and then move on through the planning process or whether the information gained during the planning process helps them to build the vision. In practice, schools will adopt different strategies for building the vision depending on their own particular circumstances. Other key processes include building budgetary and evaluation processes which are important in the planning cycle. Also, the key aspect of working with governors, staff, parents and the community in the planning process is paramount in successful planning and implementation. We have chosen (for clarity of presentation) to cover all these activities that support school planning in a companion volume *Supporting Strategic Development in Schools: Key Processes*, Routledge, 1999. Therefore, the reader is encouraged in this first book to build an understanding of the new planning model which will then be supported by the companion volume which undertakes a detailed consideration of the key processes of managing effective development in schools.

We would say, in concluding this first chapter, that the move to greater school autonomy, combined with rapid changes in the nature of learning technologies, has created demands for schools to be innovative and flexible in their responses. We believe that the planning framework outlined in this book will contribute to that process. We wish our readers well as they work their way through the ideas and concepts in the book and look forward to hearing of their responses to it.

Note

1 See for example the Times Educational Supplement (TES 1997) and Professor Brian Caldwell (1997: 360)

References

Broadhead, P., Cuckle, P., Hodgson, J. and Dunford, J. (1996) 'Improving Primary Schools through School Development Planning', in *Education Management and Administration* Vol. 24 No. 3: 277–290.

Caldwell, B. J. (1997) 'The Future of Public Education', in *Education Management and Administration* Vol. 25 No. 4: 357–370.

Davies, B. and Ellison, L. (1992) *School Development Planning*, Harlow: Longman.

DES (1989) *Planning for School Development: Advice for Governors, Headteachers and Teachers*, London: HMSO.

DES (1991) *Development Planning: A Practical Guide*, London: DES.

Giles, C. (1997) *School Development Planning: A Practical Guide to the Strategic Management Process*, Plymouth: Northcote House.

Gunter, H. (1997) *Rethinking Education: The Consequences of Jurassic Management*, London: Cassell.

Hargreaves, D. and Hopkins, D. (1991) *The Empowered School: The Management and Practice of Development Planning*, London: Cassell.

MacGilchrist, B., Mortimore, P., Savage, J. and Beresford, C., (1995) *Planning Matters: The Impact of Development Planning in Primary Schools*, London: Paul Chapman Publishing.

Mintzberg, H. (1994) *The Rise and Fall of Strategic Planning*, Hemel Hempstead: Prentice Hall.

National Audit Office (1994) *Value for Money at Grant-maintained Schools: A Review of Performance*, London: HMSO.

Puffitt, R., Stoten, B. and Winkley, D. (1992) *Business Planning for Schools*, Harlow: Longman.

Skelton, M., Reeves, G. and Playfoot, D. (1991) *Development Planning for Primary Schools*, Windsor: NFER.

Times Educational Supplement 2 (1997) 'Prehistoric Pretensions' 28.02.97.

West, M. and Ainscow, M. (1991) *Managing School Development: A Practical Guide*, London: Fulton.

Chapter 2

The evolution of the new model
Rethinking school planning

This chapter shares with the reader how our current thinking has developed to take school planning forward well into the twenty-first century. It acts as an executive summary to provide a strategic overview of the models which we have worked through over the last few years and provides an holistic view of the detail that follows in the succeeding chapters. We examine here three models of planning. We outline briefly the original model that we articulated in 1992, then examine the need for schools to move from short-term school development planning to longer-term strategic perspectives and, most significantly, to incorporate a 'futures thinking' perspective. The third model, which we then go on to develop in this book, adds the concept of strategic intent in order that the planning process is more responsive to the needs of a dynamic environment.

1992: The original model

Our original work (Davies and Ellison 1992: 9) considered that planning should take a mainly operational perspective with a one-year plan being extended up to two or three years. At the time, many schools considered that only certain major activities such as curriculum and staffing needed planning but we felt that a broader planning framework was necessary. We considered the school development plan to be the mechanism for defining a school's aims and translating them into effective education. We sub-divided activities into *core elements* (representing the main purpose of the school) and *support elements* (which facilitate the effective operation of the core elements). Following extensive work with schools and Local Education Authorities (LEAs), we created a model to show our view of the way in which the elements built up into the school development plan:

The model which we proposed brought all the separate activities together into one coherent document in order to 'provide a strategic picture of where the school is, where it is going and how it intends to

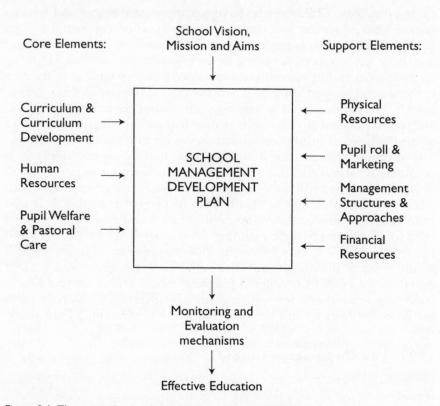

Core Elements:

School Vision,
Mission and Aims

Support Elements:

Curriculum &
Curriculum
Development

Human
Resources

Pupil Welfare
& Pastoral
Care

SCHOOL
MANAGEMENT
DEVELOPMENT
PLAN

Physical
Resources

Pupil roll &
Marketing

Management
Structures &
Approaches

Financial
Resources

Monitoring and
Evaluation
mechanisms

Effective Education

Figure 2.1 The original school development planning model.
Source: Davies and Ellison 1992: 9, Financial Times Management.

get there' (Davies and Ellison 1992: 9). While we also proposed separate, more detailed plans for each of the areas shown in Figure 2.1, their integration ensured that the separate plans would be complementary.

There is now a wider range of decisions taken at the school level and a wider range of options available with regard to strategic direction and more operational matters but much of the planning emphasis has still been on the creation of development plans setting out the school's proposed activities over a one- to three-year period. Considerable expertise has developed at the school level with revisions taking place to both the layout and the planning process but this approach has encouraged incrementalism rather than a more creative approach. The tendency to short-termism has also been exacerbated in schools by a sense of being out of control of the change process because of government legislation.

Although our 1992 work on school development planning was successful in establishing benchmarks of good planning practice, the rate of economic, technological and educational change has gathered pace during the 1990s. Children who have recently started school and who go on to higher education will complete their education between the years 2013 and 2020. What is more, they could be working with technologies that have not yet been invented in an organisation that has yet to be created. What sort of educational experience will they have over the next ten years and beyond? How will schools plan to operate in this environment? The continued and increasingly rapid changes in both the global and the educational environments require that schools should think ahead about the types of institutions which they wish to be in ten years' time.

It is important to take a longer term holistic perspective which considers what the nature of learning and the learning technology will be like in the twenty-first century and to avoid an incremental approach whereby a school would gradually alter its current provision. It is also wise to avoid some of the mistakes of industry and commerce where a rigid approach to strategic planning (as discussed by Mintzberg 1994) has produced inflexibility and an inability to grasp opportunities which would ensure the long-term effectiveness of the organisation. Our conclusion was that the original planning model which we had articulated was appropriate for the shorter-term operational planning cycle but it needed to be set in a reconceptualised, wider-reaching framework.

1995: The three-stage model

We believed that a more appropriate model to the incremental approach would be to use futures thinking in order to develop a vision about a desired future state and then to create scenarios which might represent the school's future. Senior managers in schools could then use the process of strategic planning to complement and extend the existing development planning process. The link between these three activities can be seen in Figure 2.2.

We undertook a research project (Davies and Ellison 1997b) aimed at investigating the extent to which schools were moving to this form of thinking. The project used a survey methodology with a sample consisting of 40 schools from across England. These were schools that had previously worked with us on establishing development planning processes and had an initial capability in this area. The following sections outline the key characteristics of each of the stages of the 1995 model and report on the findings of the survey which related to each stage.

I Futures thinking

Although it is not possible to know precisely what the future will bring, current trends and indicators can help to provide useful insights to

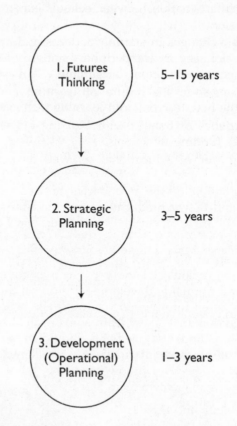

Figure 2.2 The three-stage model.
Source: after Davies and Ellison 1997a: 76.

develop a reasonably credible perspective. Therefore, by examining trends and building scenarios of possible future outcomes we can develop a futures perspective.

When attempting to develop a view of the school and of the process of learning in the next century, it is useful to consider some of the trends and thinking that will impact on schools. An articulation of some of these trends and thinking can be seen in the work of Beare and Slaughter (1993), Gerstner *et al.* (1994), Handy (1994), Hargreaves (1994), and Caldwell (1997). A useful summary is provided by Davies (1997) who considers the trends that are already evident but which will become of increasing importance over the next five to fifteen years:

- Relating value-added educational gains to resource levels allows schools to be compared in terms of 'value for money'. There will be pressure to increase performance with the same resource level.

- Increased differentiation between schools encourages more specialised provision.
- Considerable changes in staffing patterns and arrangements, more
  para-professionals, core and periphery staff, fixed-term performance-
  led contracts, school-site pay bargaining.
- Radical changes in the nature of teaching and learning as the
  impact of the new teaching and learning technologies gathers pace.
- Greater varieties of finance with blurring between state-only and
  private-only funding of schools.
- Contracting out of educational as well as service elements of
  schooling.
- A re-examination of the boundaries between different stages of
  education and between education and the community.

(adapted from Davies 1997: 20–21)

The senior leaders of the school must develop insights about the future
and then lead the various stakeholders (such as governors, community,
staff, parents and pupils) in developing an idea of the type of provision
which will be offered into the next century. The benefits can be seen of
not having a senior management team who are all alike; a range of views
and some tensions and disagreements should be seen as beneficial. A
range of stakeholders, both internal and external, need to be involved in
developing this perspective, although much of the work will be carried
out by the senior management team and the governors. It may be useful
to have a formal 'futures' group encompassing a range of stakeholders.

The evidence of futures thinking in schools

Only seven (17 per cent) of the sample of 40 schools acknowledged that
they were involved in any type of futures thinking. Of those which had
considered futures thinking, this had been at the instigation of heads or
deputies who had been on innovative courses which had involved
major sections on scenario building and futures thinking. In the
remainder of the schools there was no evidence of planning or futures
thinking beyond five years. This was despite the fact that the pupils
had a five- to seven-year career in many of the schools and many of the
staff had a 20-year career there. Of the seven schools that had involved
themselves in futures thinking:

- Four schools had spent time writing scenarios describing what the
  school might be like at some point in the twenty-first century.
- Two had constructed lists of the key features which they expected
  to be apparent in the early stages of the twenty-first century.

- One head described her vision of educational provision for a particular group of children in a large centre of population.

Of the remaining 33 schools, there was little or no evidence of this type
of thinking taking place although five of these schools responded that
they recognised the importance of futures thinking and hoped to 'get
round to it soon'. With the explosion of interest in the new technologies
that will dominate much of the education and learning practice in the
next century, this was a very disturbing finding.

2 Strategic planning

Strategic planning is the process of matching the school's activities to the
emerging environment, bearing in mind what can feasibly be achieved
with the resource base which can be generated. Before formalising the
plan, the two processes of strategic analysis and choice are undertaken.
The aim of strategic analysis is to gain an understanding of the strategic
position of the school and the environment in which it must operate as
this will affect the choice of strategy. To appreciate fully the strategic
position of the school it is necessary to understand how a wide range of
stakeholders, such as pupils, staff, employers, governors and the community, view the situation which the school faces and its possible direction. The information will usually be assembled by the senior
management team. Strategic choice involves the identification or
generation of options, the evaluation of those options and the selection
of appropriate strategies. The final decision on choices would normally
be made by the governors and the senior management team.

The evidence of strategic planning in schools

Only five of the schools had considered a longer-term (five-year) formal
planning process. The remainder still focused on short-term incremental
plans. More significantly, three of these five schools had formed five-year
plans as a result of a specific external demand (either increased pupil
intake or Technology College Status) and not as part of the standard
planning process.

Very significantly, only one school had considered the financial future
over a five-year time scale using projected activities and their costs set
against likely pupil roll and, hence, estimated income trends. This was a
curious finding, in that while most schools have some knowledge of
pupil numbers over a three- to five-year period, these numbers have not
been incorporated into a financial and planning model.

In most schools it was evident that reactive and incremental thinking
predominated and that this was not linked to a futures perspective.

Schools made similar types of comments about the difficulty of planning outside the annual budgeting cycle. This is in the context of many of the pupils having three to five years remaining in the school but their need only being analysed on an annual basis.

In summary, we found an almost total absence of strategic planning over this time scale.

3 Operational school development planning

This is the critical stage at which those within the school develop a plan for achieving the options which have been chosen. There should be realism about the balance between new developments and the maintenance of the existing activities otherwise there will be work overload and a lack of resources. If the plans are to come to fruition, it is important to consider both the process of creating the development plan and the nature of the document itself.

In too many cases, the plan has become so detailed and unwieldy that it cannot be used as a working document. It should, therefore, be set out in an easily read format and cover more than just the curriculum, finance, staffing and staff development. In our 1992 book we suggested that schools should also cover management structures and approaches, pupil welfare and pastoral care, pupil roll and marketing, physical resources, monitoring and evaluation. Included in the documentation would be costings for each activity and named responsibility for the achievement of the specified outcomes. Review arrangements should be clear so that problems or additional resource needs can be identified and successes can be recognised.

It is important to consider the role of the various partners in formulating and implementing operational plans. While governors and senior managers are extensively involved in the more strategic aspects of planning, the staff and pupils will need to be more deeply involved in operational planning. Normally, a planning group or senior team will be overseeing the operational planning process which turns the strategic decisions into action and which ensures the maintenance of the school's ongoing activities. There will need to be frequent communications between school groups such as curricular areas, key stage teams, school council and support staff, so that the activities and targets which are written into the plan are realistic and appropriate as well as contributing to the achievement of the overall objectives of the school.

The evidence of operational development planning in schools

All 40 schools reported that they had development plans, with several quoting the Office for Standards in Education (OFSTED) process as a catalyst for bringing together curriculum and other plans into a more coherent whole school planning process. Thirteen schools had a three-year plan while the remaining 27 schools had extended their one-year plan into a second year.

Some schools indicated that a cross-school planning group (often including governors) had been responsible for putting the document together. In others the construction of the plan had fallen to the head or a deputy.

There were separate plans for each subject area and for other aspects of the school's work although the format of these sub-unit plans did not always follow that of the main plan, so that it was difficult to track the priorities through. In others, there was a clear link between whole school objectives and those in the sub-plans. In quantitative terms, 24 of the schools showed clear links where in the remaining 16 there seemed to be an ad hoc collection of sub-plans and total plans which had very little inter-relationship.

Most schools had found the headings of core and support areas and the grid layout (which we had proposed in our earlier work) useful. As we had originally hoped, they had adapted the system to suit their own situation with extra sections added, for example 'parents and the community'.

There is a need for a system of monitoring in order to check progress towards the planned outcomes. This aspect has often been neglected in schools. We found that only 18 had detailed systems for monitoring progress. This usually involved a member of the senior management team or the governors. When questioned, the schools revealed a range of approaches such as:

- reporting (verbally or in writing) to a meeting of the senior management team (SMT) or governors on progress;
- discussion with line manager on a fortnightly basis;
- reporting termly to a nominated member of the SMT;
- governor or line manager attending team meetings to make a judgement about progress.

One school had used a database to enter targets, dates, responsible person and name of person who would monitor progress. This seemed complex but enabled the information to be printed out according to name, target or due date for ease of use.

Reflections

In general we have witnessed greater sophistication in school planning since our early work in 1992. We were interested to see that our earlier model, which we had developed through partnerships with schools, had led to much useful work. All schools in our survey had plans which extended over two years with several being extended over three. We found, however, that most schools had not, in the intervening time, moved forwards themselves to consider more long-term approaches to direction-setting. The approaches which we found were, on the whole, incremental. With the rapid changes in the economy and society together with the revolution in teaching and learning offered by the new learning technologies it would seem very desirable that more fundamental long-term thinking should take place.

The initial three-stage model has proved useful in identifying the concepts of futures thinking, strategic planning and shorter-term operational development planning. However, even if schools do take on a more strategic planning function, there is still a problem of applying this process in an era of rapid change. A reliance on strategic planning assumes a rational and predictable process which, in practice may not be possible in the current turbulent environment. It may also tend to be very incremental, despite what its proponents say. We therefore sought an alternative perspective for the next phase of our research project.

1998: Refining the model – alternative perspectives

In one of the most outstanding pieces which we have read on the topic of coping with a turbulent environment, Max Boisot (1995) provides two key areas of analysis in his chapter 'Preparing for turbulence: the changing relationship between strategy and management development in the learning organisation'. He suggests that the traditional strategic planning approach is ineffective because of the turbulence caused by rapidly increasing rates of change. He identifies four basic types of response: strategic planning, emergent strategy, intrapreneurship and strategic intent. We deal with these concepts in detail in Chapter 4, but in this summary we will just discuss strategic planning and strategic intent.

The success of *strategic planning* is based on there being a predictable environment which can be identified so that appropriate strategies can be implemented in a rational, steady way. The rate of change is assumed to be less than the organisation's ability to understand and adapt to those changes. In the educational context, rapid change over the last ten years and the future impact of technology on learning have cast doubt as to whether strategic planning over a three- to five-year period is possible for all of a school's activities.

Strategic intent is an approach which seems to have a lot to offer to those in schools, as an alternative to traditional strategic planning. Boisot believes that an organisation 'operating in a regime of strategic intent can use a common vision to keep the behaviour of its employees aligned with a common purpose when it decentralises in response to turbulence' (1995: 37). This is a very powerful way of linking futures thinking and strategy in order to provide direction and purpose for an organisation as it takes account of high levels of turbulence but maintains high levels of understanding of the core direction needed.

Creating a new model for educational applications

In using Boisot's model in our work with headteachers, we have found they find concepts of strategic planning and strategic intent particularly valuable in thinking about planning in schools. They see that part of their activities are stable and predictable, for example a group of pupils on entering a school will stay for a number of years and they have to be planned for and, as such, strategic planning over a three- to five-year period is useful. They also recognise, however, that rapid change means that part of the planning environment is very turbulent and the appropriate response is to use strategic intent to increase the capability of the school to cope with that environment.

With strategic intent the school needs to establish a process of coping with and using the rapid change and turbulence. It does this not by detailed planning but by 'binding' the staff together in the furtherance of focused key priorities that become core activities of the organisation. We call these strategic intents. Thus, staff understand these key intents and also understand that detailed planning in the environment is not possible. This approach is appropriate in building capability in staff to meet major challenges in the future when precise plans are not available but where capability to respond in a dynamic environment is necessary. A good example is technology, where the speed of change and usage is not predictable but where developing staff competence and capability involves creating the right culture about independent learning and technology in general. Thus the school, in establishing this consensus and understanding, can be seen to move upward and to the right in the matrix on Figure 2.3.

Strategic planning, on the other hand, presents a situation where the school is trying to reduce the effect of rapid change and turbulence by controlling more of the specific details of the activity or change in question. It does this by reducing the uncertainty caused by change through increasing its understanding as it moves down from left to right in Figure 2.3 and it is able to plan more of its activities. The reason it is able to do this is either because the time frame is shorter or because the nature of the activity is more predictable. Certain parts of the school's activities, such as regular property maintenance, are examples of this. The school in these circumstances can predict likely expenditure and activities and create a strategic plan for them.

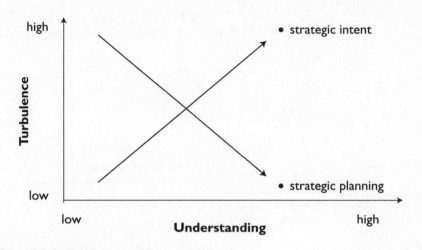

Figure 2.3 Strategic intent and strategic planning.
Source: Boisot 1995: 40.

Integrating strategic intent into the new model

We now see that schools should engage in three planning activities. First, futures thinking identifies longer-term fundamental shifts in the educational environment and provides a futures perspective. Second, following strategic analysis, a strategic intent is created for the less predictable areas of medium-term planning while traditional strategic planning is utilised for the definable and predictable areas. Third, there is one- or two-year planning which, in the UK, is in the form of the operational school development plan. Increased government emphasis on value-added performance indicators and specific outcome measures has given extra importance to the concept of target-setting and measuring the outcomes achieved. It is our view that the school development plan should take a new format, that of the operational target-setting plan. It seems appropriate to think of planning as three activities which interact and reinforce each other, rather than being strictly hierarchical and linear.

We now move on to unpack each of the key elements of the reconceptualised model as shown in Figure 2.4.

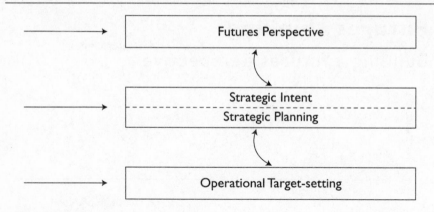

Figure 2.4 The reconceptualised model

References

Beare, H. and Slaughter, R. (1993) *Education for the Twenty First Century*, London: Routledge.

Boisot, M. (1995) 'Preparing for turbulence' in B. Garratt (ed.), *Developing Strategic Thought*, London: McGraw-Hill.

Caldwell, B. J. (1997) 'Global trends and expectations for the further reform of schools' and 'Thinking in time a gestalt for schools of the new millennium' in B. Davies and L. Ellison *School Leadership for the 21st Century: A Competency and Knowledge Approach* London: Routledge.

Davies, B. (1997) 'Rethinking the educational context: a reengineering approach' in B. Davies and L. Ellison *School Leadership for the 21st Century: A Competency and Knowledge Approach* London: Routledge.

Davies, B. and Ellison, L. (1992) *School Development Planning*, Harlow: Longman.

Davies, B. and Ellison, L. (eds) (1997a) *School Leadership for the 21st Century: A Competency and Knowledge Approach* London: Routledge.

Davies, B. and Ellison, L (1997b) 'Futures and strategic perspectives in school planning', Paper presented at the American Educational Research Association Annual Meeting, Chicago, March.

Gerstner, L. V., Semerad, R. D., Doyle, D. P. and Johnson, W. B. (1994) *Reinventing Education: America's Public Schools*, New York: Dutton.

Handy, C. (1994) *The Empty Raincoat: Making Sense of the Future*, London: Hutchinson.

Hargreaves, D. (1994) *The Mosaic of Learning: Schools and Teachers for the New Century*, London: Demos.

Mintzberg, H. (1994) *The Rise and Fall of Strategic Planning*, Hemel Hempstead: Prentice Hall.

Chapter 3

Futures thinking

Building a futures perspective

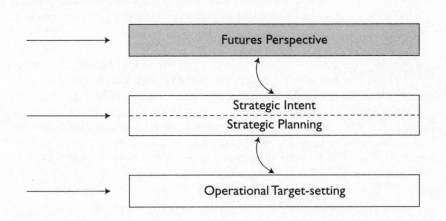

Introduction

The first dimension of our reconceptualised model of school planning involves using futures thinking to build a 'futures perspective'. This requires the *leadership* capacity of 'looking outside' or 'looking to the horizon' which is fundamental to setting the direction of an organisation and contrasts with the *management* priority of co-ordinating current activities. Futures thinking involves the school leader in standing back from the traditional operational and incremental thinking approaches and analysing broad global and national trends which are likely to impact on education over the next ten to fifteen years. The leader must then start to build in the school the capacity or 'mindset' to interpret and understand the significance of these trends for the school. This is a radical agenda for school leaders. Peter Drucker, a management writer who is highly respected for his predictions of trends sees the challenge as follows:

What will be taught and learned; how it will be taught and learned; who will make use of schooling; and the position of the school in society – all of this will change greatly during the ensuing decades. Indeed, no other institution faces challenges as radical as those that will transform the school.

(1993: 209)

He sets this in a more fundamental shift within society:

Every few hundred years in Western history there occurs a sharp transformation.... . Within a few short decades, society rearranges itself ... its world view; its basic values; its social and political structures.... . We are currently living through such a transformation.
(Drucker 1993: 1)

This would suggest that schools need to develop the ability to identify and plan for fundamental changes in the way they carry out their role. Schools are, however, places where the organisational history and culture make it notoriously difficult to bring about change. If we are to do more than respond to immediate policy changes or current crises we need to identify potential trends, consider possible future scenarios and, above all, build reflective learning communities which can adapt to whatever challenges or opportunities arise. This involves agreeing and living a set of values as a benchmark and building a set of learning skills so that opportunities can be shaped and taken rather than the school being the victim of unforeseen changes and events.

All organisations must see the need to reappraise fundamentally what they are doing as a result of changes in the global economy. Schools are no exception. Hammer and Champy (1993) listed three factors that were forcing companies to change their current practices: the nature of global *competition;* the nature of *customers;* the nature of the *change* process itself. These are dealt with in more detail in the next section. Books such as Bill Gates' *The Road Ahead* (1995) and Tom Cannon's *Welcome to the Revolution: Managing Paradox in the 21st Century* (1996) are popular expressions of how profound is the change that we face. The trends drawn from the business world are paralleled by writers from the expanding literature on 'futures thinking' in education. Beare and Slaughter (1993: 108) contend that 'rapid change means that many past assumptions, meanings and purposes are no longer valid and self-evident.'

The rest of this chapter will put forward ideas which we hope leaders will use to change mindsets so that the school can respond to the needs of the future. We look first, therefore, at the nature of the changes we face and, second, at the work of four writers, Hammer and Champy (1993), Dent (1995) and Handy (1994), who have developed new perspectives to change 'mindsets' to enable us to think about the future. Third, we move on to consider what all this means for education and suggest ten ways in which individual schools, education systems or, most importantly, pupil learning might be reengineered.

The nature of the changes

It is possible to examine the nature of the changes which we are witnessing in two ways: (i) by examining global economic and social trends; (ii) by analysing current educational trends. This should allow schools to begin to see how they may need to develop in order to be effective in the future.

Examining global economic and social trends

Hammer and Champy (1993) highlighted three factors that are driving the global reengineering movement: competition, customers and change. What is happening in the global goods and services market in terms of *competition*? The expansion of world trade and the reduction of tariff barriers through the GATT (General Agreement on Trade and Tariffs) process have resulted in competition on a global scale. This globalisation of economic activity has meant that an individual nation state can no longer isolate itself from this intense competition. The rise of the Pacific Rim, articulated in books such as John Naisbitt's 'Megatrends Asia' (1996), has focused attention on the competitive challenge faced by traditional western economies, especially from the emergence of China. In addition, there is the competition from the low wage Eastern European economies. Reich (1992) suggests that there will be three types of jobs in the future: highly paid jobs associated with information-based occupations; assembly and manufacturing jobs; and low-paid local jobs such as those in restaurants and hairdressers. Global competition effectively exports the second category of jobs. As a result it has a profound impact on the future of our children. Unless they develop high quality thinking, problem-solving and technological skills to compete with the best in the world, they will be competing for the low wage/low skill local jobs. Even these could disappear quite soon. Fast food chains are geared up to offer 'staff-free' catering environments as soon as costing factors and social factors make this appropriate. Minor incremental change is inadequate to meet this competitive challenge and what is needed is a much more fundamental rethinking about how our organisations operate in this competitive climate.

The second factor, that of the *customers*, is centred on the increasing power of customers within global market economies and their ability to demand quality and fast response times. We are moving from a mass market approach to a quality approach aimed at individual customers. Many changes can be seen in the nature of these customers. They have experienced quality and good service and expect more and better quality in the future. They are better informed, having more data on which to make their decisions, and know their legal rights in cases of dispute. They are less deferential and dictate what they want, when they want it and how they want to pay for it. Customers want to be seen as individuals and to receive a customised product and they are aware that there is a plentiful supply of goods and services so that they can pick and choose. They are even demanding 'more for less' in an attempt to obtain good value for money. The result is a reorientation of producers' attitudes to customers in the business sector and the development of new operating methods to be able to provide the customers with what they want when they want it. This is also being reflected in attempts to make public sector activities such as education more responsive and to provide 'more for less'. Thus schools are facing pressure from the publication of league tables of performance and from open enrolment policies that seek to give the customers of education more information and power. If customers are unable to obtain the goods or services which they require from the traditional supplier, they will go elsewhere – as many providers of education are beginning to discover.

Finally, there is the nature of *change* itself, driven by technological change, especially in the knowledge and information sphere. Change is being driven by the rapid transfer of information facilitated by the new technologies and is presenting a context in which it is both constant, rapid and fundamental. The shift is from the traditional definition of the factors of production being land, labour and capital to one in which Drucker (1993: 33) sees that 'knowledge is fast becoming the sole factor of production, sidelining both capital and labor'. For those of us employed in the knowledge industry, the implications are profound. The key points to consider are:

- change has become pervasive, persistent and normal;
- there is an accelerating rate of technological advance;
- the business cycle and the economic cycle are no longer predictable; and thus
- the nature of work, the economy and employment in the future are also uncertain;
- all products have shorter life-cycles, reducing from years to months.

The result of these three factors, competition, customers and change, is to drive the development of new forms of organisation and new patterns of careers. The nature of employment is driven by the rise of the virtual organisation, where core staff link through a series of networks (both interpersonal and technological) to deliver a service or a product. Individuals can no longer look forward to one career with one organisation but will have a number of jobs and at any one time may have a 'portfolio' of jobs. Caldwell and Haywood (1998) draw out a number of economic and social trends that will impact over the next few years:

1   That because of the explosion of knowledge and the pervasive and penetrating influence of information technology, the world in the twenty-first century will be fundamentally different from the past.
2   That most of the opportunities for our young people in the future will be in knowledge-based work.
3   That for the developed nations, many of their future opportunities will come through complementing, not competing with, the rapid growth of developing nations.
4   That many of these opportunities will be through the provision of knowledge-based services to firms and government agencies in developing nations, using the creativity and innovation of their young people.
5   That the key economic resources for the developed nations will be the knowledge and intellect of their young people, being even more important than commodities and natural resources.
6   That much of the conventional employment in existing industries in developed nations, especially process work in manufacturing industries, will disappear.
7   That technology will continue to drive change at a rapid rate, and diversity will be the order of the day.
8   That many opportunities for young people will be in industries and activities that have not yet been thought of, or invented, and these opportunities will continue to change.
9   That it will be essential for young people to be flexible and responsive to new opportunities as they occur.
10 That the most important capacity for our young people will be the ability to learn, and to continue to learn throughout their lifetime.
11 That information technology, including multimedia, will be an important learning aid in the future, and much of the learning will occur in informal settings, such as at home, or at work.
12 That the school will lose its monopoly in the education of our young people.

(Caldwell and Haywood 1998: 117–118)

This link between the wider societal changes and education provided by Caldwell allows us now to proceed to consider current educational trends.

Analysing current educational trends

To date, the education sector, both in the UK and overseas has witnessed a number of changes and trend patterns. We would summarise
these as:

- *The establishment of centralised curriculum and testing frameworks*
  Governments have set frameworks and benchmarks within which
  their education systems must operate. The management concept of
  'loose-tight' frameworks is one that has been set in place within the
  education sector. The 'tight' part is the centralised curriculum and
  testing, with the 'loose' part being that of decentralised management. Examples of this are shown in the UK and in places as far
  away as Victoria in Australia.
- *Radical changes in the nature of learning and teaching* The new
  learning technologies are now starting to have a radical impact
  on pupils' learning. These technologies are not just seen in the
  school but are providing significant learning opportunities outside
  the normal school environment and structure. They are putting
  the learner at the centre of the learning process, instead of the
  teacher.
- *Increasing emphasis on lifelong learning and the school as part of the
  community*   Government policies and local initiatives are promoting wider access to educational opportunities and the re-entry to
  education. This is part of a culture in which individuals have
  several jobs in a lifetime and need access to regular skills and
  professional updating.
- *Increased differentiation between educational institutions* The Education Reform Act led to a focus on differentiation between schools
  based on type of governance and management. This resulted in
  locally managed schools, grant-maintained schools and City Technology Colleges. This structural differentiation is maintained in
  government proposals (DFEE 1997) which recommend a realign-
  ment into community, aided and foundation schools. This differentiation has, in the past, diverted attention away from a more
  significant differentiation which is between schools and the types
  of clients for which they cater, for example through the continued
  development of technology or language or other specialised provision. The White Paper begins to attack this problem, referring to the
  need to extend the provision of specialist schools and to take their
  work further out into the community.
- *Enhanced levels of parental choice* While it has always been true that
  choice is limited by the availability of places and the parents'
  ability to transport their children, it is nevertheless true that

many parents have been able to have an effective choice between schools. This choice is being further enhanced by the differentiation between schools and the ability of technology to provide alternatives to traditional schooling.

- *Greater varieties of funding sources*   The simple distinction between state-only funding or private funding of education is beginning to blur and break down. In the higher education sector, the phasing out of student grants and the introduction of student loans and charges for tuition have altered radically the ideal of free access to higher education. The previous government's assisted places and nursery voucher schemes could be seen as attempts at a 'mixed economy' of funding. The Private Finance Initiative can also be seen as an attempt to build both a rhetoric and practice of funding public services.

- *Greater accountability at the institutional level*   This has been evident in the testing process at the ages of 7, 11, 14, 16 and 18 and the subsequent publication of the outcomes for a school as Key Stage, GCSE and A level results. Performance measures have also been considerably increased by the OFSTED process and the publication of the inspection reports. The threat of being named as a 'failing school' and the possibility of closure increase the pressure on schools. The government's insistence (DFEE 1997) that each school should demonstrate year-on-year increases in pupil attainment reinforces the accountability of the school for the effective provision of education.

- *Focus on value-added*   The debate on how much added value a school provides has been given increased emphasis as more children pass through the key age stages, and comparative data for the same group of children at those stages can be obtained. This can be laid alongside the data for the relative costs of that performance. When balancing factors are taken into account, valuable information can be available for parents, the wider community and those who control the funding of schools.

- *Considerable changes in staffing patterns*   We have witnessed the increase in the number of what could be called 'para-professionals' who support the teacher and school in a number of ways. In addition, schools have been driven to provide flexibility in staffing so that some staff have long-term permanent appointments but others undertake duties for a limited period of time. The growth of fixed-term contracts has also been paralleled by the growth of performance-related contracts, especially for senior managers in schools.

If, in 1988, the reader had been asked to look at trends and identify the points that might emerge by 1998 would the above trends have been discernible? Some were evident, such as the moves towards self-managing schools which originated in the schemes of local financial management in several areas; others were not so obvious. Even with financial management, the precise details and implications were not predictable. It is the consideration of possible trends and scenarios that builds capability to think about the future and all of the examples referred to above were in the realms of possibility ten years ago even if their final form was not clear. We now need to develop new and creative ways of thinking about the future.

Three perspectives on changing mindsets

How do we take a fresh look at our situation? Three useful perspectives are provided by Hammer and Champy (1993), Dent (1995) and Handy (1994). They are, respectively, reengineering, left and right brain thinking and the Sigmoid curve.

Reengineering

Hammer and Champy first articulated the concept of reengineering in 1993 in order to explain the type of rethinking that was necessary in organisations to deal with the radical change in the nature of the global market. They defined reengineering as:

> the *fundamental rethinking* and *radical redesign* of *business processes* to achieve *dramatic improvement* in critical contemporary measures of performance.
>
> (Hammer and Champy 1993: 32; our italics)

It is worth spending a little time unpacking each of these elements. Firstly, reengineering is about fundamental rethinking. It avoids the incremental approach and starts with the proverbial 'clean sheet of paper' to reconceptualise the processes and their context. This links into the second element, that of radical redesign. Reengineering makes the assumption that past and current processes are inadequate so, while it is important to research why they are inadequate, more emphasis should be given to radical new solutions. Third, there is the key aspect of business processes (which in educational terms would equate to learning processes). Hammer and Stanton (1995: 17) consider that: 'The verb "to reengineer" takes as its object a business process and nothing else. We reengineer how work is done, how outputs are created from inputs. We cannot and do not reengineer organisational units.'

The fourth element, dramatic improvement, is concerned not with making things 5 or 10 per cent better but with achieving dramatic leaps in performance.

It is important that reengineering is not seen as restructuring, so that one set of organisational structures is replaced with another. The key questions are not about how departments or organisational units are re-sorted, but about which processes create value for the customer and which organisational functions support them. Writers such as Carr and Johansson (1995) concur with this interpretation of reengineering in that they see the 'three pillars' of reengineering as: process focus, radical change and dramatic improvement. Reengineers would be concerned with learning processes and radical solutions that challenge existing patterns of operation. Thus, in the education world, we should be considering how pupils learn and not restructuring the organisational units of the school. One of the educational outcomes of this form of thinking could be that some of the effective learning in the future will be technology-based and take place outside the normal school building or structures.

Left and right brain thinking

How do we go about developing this reengineering mindset? Dent (1995) proposes that, in seeking to find ways of responding in a dynamic environment, we should examine left and right brain thinking. He distinguishes between them thus:

LEFT BRAIN	RIGHT BRAIN
• repetitive	• creative
• complex	• complex
• computational work	• intuitive powers and judgement

(Dent 1995: 12)

He believes that the 'left brain' characteristics have served us adequately to date but that there is now a need for a greater emphasis on right brain thinking. He goes on to suggest that it is possible to use the concept of halves of the brain being very different to characterise incremental and radical innovators in the following ways:

Incremental innovators	Radical innovators
Tend to:	Tend to:
• rely on the left brain	• rely on the right brain
• approach problems systematically	• approach problems from new angles
• be social and competitive	• be loners
• love results, progress and feedback	• love challenges and puzzles
• operate in neat methodical environments	• operate in messy environments
• be stable and measured	• be eccentric and moody
• be more serious	• have a strong sense of humour

(Dent 1995: 269)

Dent would see the encouragement of 'right brain' radical thinking as necessary to cope with the challenge of leading in a rapidly changing environment of the twenty-first century. In developing a futures perspective it is obviously important to encourage the right brain radical thinkers but also to enhance and encourage the capability of all individuals for radical thinking.

The Sigmoid curve

A useful tool to explore the need to rethink critically future direction is provided by Charles Handy (1994), in *The Empty Raincoat: Making Sense of the Future*, who makes use of the Sigmoid curve.

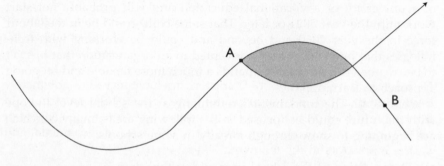

Figure 3.1 The Sigmoid curve.
Source: Handy 1994: 51.

Handy suggests that most organisations rise and fall or expand and contract in a way very similar to a sine wave. The challenge for leadership in a successful organisation is to spot when it is at point A and to reengineer so that the organisation does not rest on its laurels when it is still expanding. It must take the risk of moving onto a new Sigmoid curve and not wait to change until it is moving downwards at point B. Handy expresses this as:

> The right place to start that second curve is at point A, where there is time, as well as the resources and the energy, to get the curve through its initial explorations and floundering before the first curve begins to dip downwards. That would seem obvious; were it not for the fact that at point A all the messages coming through to the individual or the institution are that everything is going fine, that it would be folly to change when the current recipes are working so well. All that we know of change, be it personal change or change in organisations, tells us that the real energy for change only comes when you are looking disaster in the face, at point B on the first curve. At this point, however, it is going to require a mighty effort to drag oneself up to where, by now, one should be on the second curve.
>
> (Handy 1994: 51–52)

Ten key reengineering trends for schools

It would seem that the expectations of customers, the nature of competition and the ongoing rate of change itself are unlikely to leave education in a backwater. Education and training are at the forefront of society's attempts to come to terms with the new realities. It is difficult to imagine that education (especially the school sector) will not itself have to change radically. However this is only the beginning, as the child who starts school in the year 2000 has a long educational journey to the completion of a university or a vocational education and will probably not start work until the year 2021 or later. That same child could be in the labour force in the year 2060 and beyond and could be working with technologies that have not yet been invented in an organisation that has yet to be created. This scenario demands a much more flexible and on-going approach to learning.

What next? The fundamental rethinking at the school level to cope with the future could be focused in the following areas, many of which are beginning to show through already in some schools:

- Organisation of the school year and school day
- Technology and its impact on learning and schools

- Staffing
- The nature of the curriculum
- Different types of schools
- Developing a learning community rather than a school
- How teachers facilitate a learning day
- Staff skills and competencies
- Resourcing education
- Equity issues

Organisation of the school year and school day

The continued pressure on schools, especially in some London districts, to increase pupil numbers to meet parental demand will, if met by the simple strategy of extra buildings, cause an uneconomic use of capital resources. The simple fact that schools are generally open for pupils for 190 days out of 365 (52 per cent of the possible total time) and are only open for six hours out of 24 for teaching (25 per cent of daily time) means that, in total, the school buildings are open for 13 per cent of the possible time using a 365 day, 24 hour total possibility framework (see Davies 1997). To continue the solution of more capital building does not automatically seem the most effective use of resources and, if pursued, is likely to divert resources away from educational materials and teacher supply.

School Day Calculation:

School open for pupils $\dfrac{190 \text{ days}}{365 \text{ days}}$ = 52% of the days available

$\dfrac{\text{Total hours attended}}{\text{Total hours in year}}$ $\dfrac{190 \times 6\text{hrs}}{365 \times 24}$ = $\dfrac{1140}{8760}$ = 13% of time available

---

The origins of the present school calendar come from an agricultural nation which had long summer holidays so that children could help with the harvest. This is clearly no longer appropriate. Similarly, the different length of terms with different holiday times currently increase teacher and pupil stress and contribute to 'teacher burnout' rather than providing a well paced and balanced learning environment. What alternatives are available? Some of the alternatives are outlined below.

Single track all year round education

Here, the same group of pupils attend the school but with a different pattern of attendance. Dixons' City Technology College in Bradford

(11–18) operate a series of five eight-week terms with two week breaks between each term (except for the summer which has a four-week break). The feedback from an interview with the Principal, John Lewis, suggests that this reduces teacher and pupil stress and enhances learning outcomes (see Lewis 1997). Similar patterns and benefits are reported (*Guardian* 1997) by Gareth Newman of Brooke Weston City Technology College in Corby. While the adoption of such a pattern could potentially be beneficial educationally, there would be no cost reductions.

Double shift systems

Schools are already operating variants of this, where pupils operate in the building for different time slots during the day. The most common example is where part of the A level teaching is scheduled in an extended school day between normal school closure and five or six o'clock in the evening. Two more structured approaches are available. The first involves moving the lower part of the school onto an 8.30a.m. to 2.30p.m. school day and all sixth form or Years 10–13 on a 12p.m. to 6p.m. day. This needs careful scheduling around lunch time but significantly increases capacity. In the second model, two 'schools' use the same building but instead of operating for six hours a day for 190 days, they operate reduced hours for a longer number of days. That number of days would depend on how the day was split: 8am to 1pm and 1.30p.m. to 6.30p.m. or 8a.m. to 12 and 12.30p.m. to 4.30p.m.

Multi-track systems, *incorporating a move to all year round education*

There is considerable experience in the United States of 'Year-Round Education' where the National Association for Year-Round Education, headed by Dr Charles Ballinger, co-ordinates research and disseminates best practice in different patterns of school organisation which allow more than one group of pupils (called a track) to use the same facilities. Currently 2400 schools and 1.8 million pupils across 38 states are involved in year-round education. The system operates on running a number of tracks in a school. For example if there are 180 pupils in the school in six classes of 30 pupils each it could be described as operating three tracks of 60 pupils. The capacity of the school can be increased by 33.3 per cent by operating four tracks in the school and accommodating 240 pupils. The layouts (from the US system of 180 days in a school year) demonstrate how this can be done using alternative tracking models of 45 days teaching and 15 vacation (Figure 3.2) or 60 days teaching and 20 days vacation (Figure 3.3).

SAMPLE 180-DAY CALENDAR

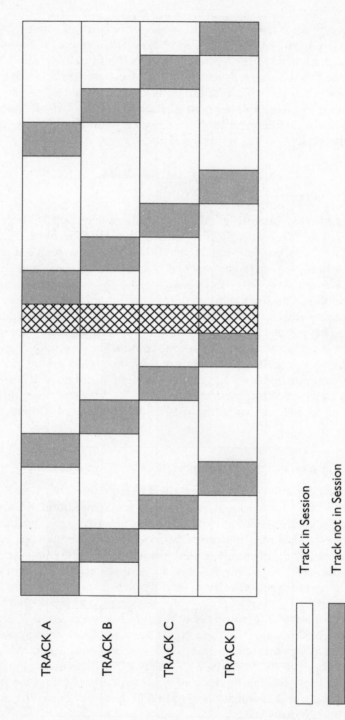

TRACK A

TRACK B

TRACK C

TRACK D

☐ Track in Session

▨ Track not in Session

▩ Winter vacations (includes entire student body)

Figure 3.2 A 45–15 Multi-track plan (four tracks).

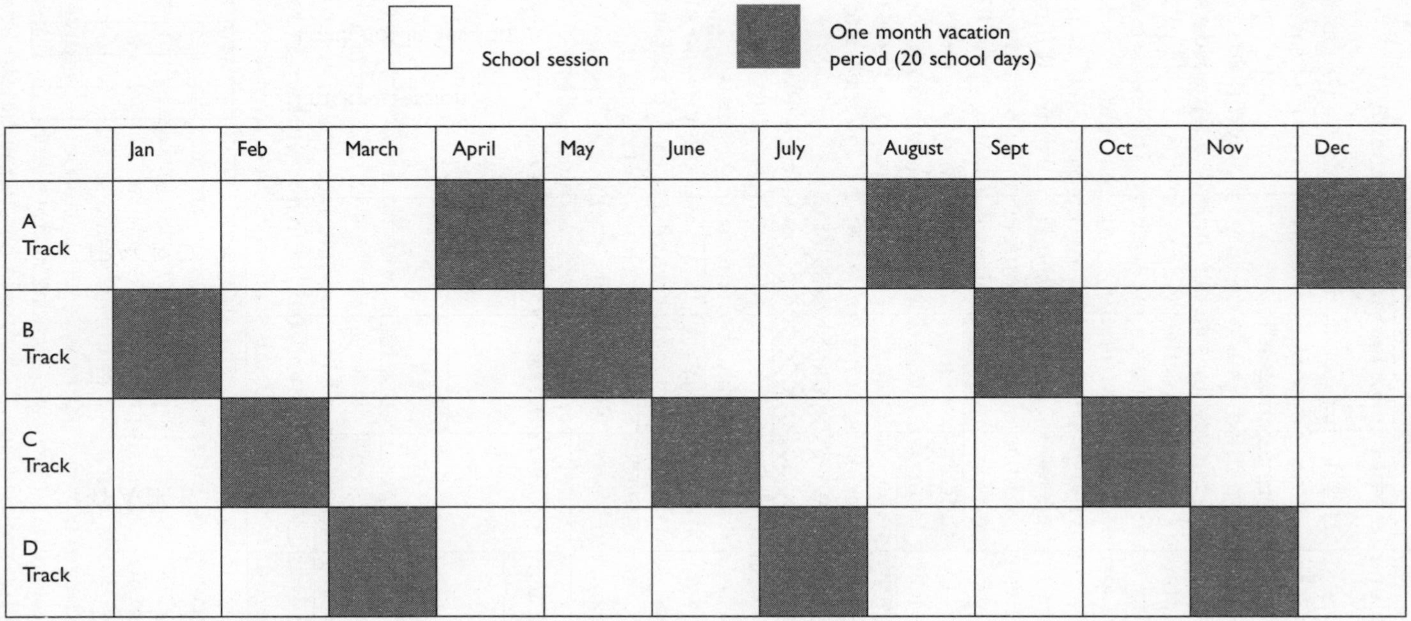

	Jan	Feb	March	April	May	June	July	August	Sept	Oct	Nov	Dec
A Track				■				■				■
B Track	■				■				■			
C Track		■				■				■		
D Track			■				■				■	

Legend:
☐ School session
■ One month vacation period (20 school days)

Figure 3.3 A 60–20 Multi-track plan (four tracks).

Technology and its impact on learning and schools

Allied to the structural changes outlined above that would seek to achieve enhanced learning outcomes and significant cost savings, there are changes to the learning process itself. Two trends, both separate and interlinked, can be identified. One is the impact of technology. Southorn (1997) explains how a Shropshire school is linked to Gwynedd's distance learning centre and uses interactive video conferencing and CD-ROM technology to teach a wider range of A-levels. This uses one hour of teacher time per week instead of the traditional four hours and has produced an improved pass rate, showing the potential of technology to replace traditional teaching at traditional times in traditional class-rooms. Similarly, Dettman's (1997) example of laptops demonstrated how this use of the technology can enhance learning. This then poses the question 'Do students have to be in school every day of the week or can they be using technology-based learning at home or in the commu-nity out of traditional school hours?' Several secondary schools now have 100+ multi-media machines, many linked to the Internet, and learning resource centres are replacing traditional libraries.

The impact of technology on learning, however, is likely to be much more radical. It threatens the very existence of the school itself. Hargreaves (1997) suggests that parents with access to high quality technology will look increasingly to home schooling as an alternative to traditional schools. Why should a pupil go to a traditional school when he/she can attend a technology centre, work at home, engage in Internet tuition, etc.? Even within schools, traditional teacher-led lessons are likely to exist for only part of the week with the emphasis switching to pupil-led activities using technology and other learning resources.

Staffing

Brent's uncle, who started work for a printing firm when he was 14, is now 64 and due to retire in a year's time. Apart from a break for National Service, to spend all one's working life with one firm is a pattern that is unlikely to be repeated by many workers in the future. Indeed the age at which individuals start work has increased and the age at which they retire has decreased. The employment pattern for many staff will encompass initial periods of temporary employment, work on short-term contracts and holding a portfolio of jobs when they enter early retirement. The standard career track no longer seems to hold sway. How do we manage staffing in schools? One way to think of reengineered employment patterns is to see teachers as individual con-tractors who contract to do specific jobs in the school for a specific time period for a reward package. This would conflict with traditional views of a job for life and a salary progression based on becoming older. If we have flexible budgets that adjust with the number of pupils, then staffing flexibility on the supply side is an organisational necessity. The challenge is to find ways to empower teachers to be responsible for their own career and salary management rather than them being participants of a bureaucratic staffing regime.

The other changing feature of employment patterns for staff is the mix between teaching and support staff. In other public sector professions, such as health care, there has been a significant growth in the range and number of para-professionals who now assist the doctor. Indeed many of the tasks traditionally undertaken by the doctor are now undertaken by these para-professionals. In education, a radical reappraisal of teaching and support staff has to take place. Either we pay teachers more in an era of fixed budgets – thus to do so we must have fewer of them – or we free them up to manage the key task of teaching and learning by getting others to do more of the routine tasks. This can mean more than the extension of the traditional nursery nurse or teacher's aide in the primary sector or laboratory or technical assistant in the secondary sector. We should be considering different levels of teaching where 'master teachers' direct teaching assistants who have different salary structures. Utilising human and technical resources should become the task of the 'master teacher' in the search for increased learning outcomes. A new grade of standard and master teacher might be established. Thus, instead of seeing teaching as a 40-year career, we should see different career patterns. Some teachers will spend a long time in post, some will leave for different careers while some will use teaching as part of a portfolio of other jobs.

The nature of the curriculum

The dilemma of any national curriculum is the one of setting up frameworks while at the same time providing flexibility and encouraging individual flair and responsiveness. The initial constraints of the UK's national curriculum have now been reduced. This leads on to the interesting point in an increasingly globalised information system as to whether the parameters of a limited national curriculum base are sufficient to deal with the knowledge explosion both in terms of content and access. Ohmae (1995) provides an example from the higher education world by taking Keio University's experimental Fujisawa campus in Japan as a forerunner of the new global education world:

> Because [all students] are on-line, they can offer real-time reactions and contributions to the curriculum, to the structure of their own programs of study, to the content of their courses, and to the quality

of their instructors. If they need information to supplement a text they are reading or a report they are writing, they can track it down through the Internet. If they want to consult an expert anywhere in the world, they can reach him or her the same way.... They have stopped being passive consumers of an educational experience defined, shaped, and evaluated by the Ministry of Education. The technology has allowed them, in a most non-Japanese fashion, to become definers and shapers and evaluators – and questioners – themselves.

(Ohmae 1995: 36)

What is an isolated pioneer in one decade tends to become commonplace in another. Thus the opportunity for students and schools to access 'the best of the best' in curriculum in global terms is rapidly becoming a reality. Two of the schools with which we work – Goff's School in Hertfordshire, England, and Gladstone Park Secondary College in Victoria, Australia – regularly benchmark their language teaching and pupil outcomes against each other as a way of obtaining a view on international standards.

Different types of schools

Parity of esteem has always been the bugbear of the English education system. The debate about selection at 11 has been as much about the effectiveness and desirability of such a process as the impossibility of ensuring parity of esteem between the resulting different schools. Initiatives such as technology colleges and schools and the language and arts schools have created a small breach in the uniformity of education provision. However, a much more radical reengineering of school provision would be achieved by the loose-tight framework where schools could choose a higher percentage of their curricula while still delivering the core elements of the National Curriculum. Thus, an emphasis between schools on different aspects of the curriculum could become much more radical, giving real choice to students and their parents while encouraging innovation within schools.

An even more radical scenario has been described by Hargreaves (1997: 11–16) who sees the school sector fracturing into:

- Private schools, forming an elite group based on traditional academic curricula;
- Specialist schools, which are technology-based and which provide high quality focused education
- Custodial schools, found largely in the inner cities and providing basic education only, thus keeping pupils off the streets;

- Home schooling, which will expand because of the support provided by the information revolution.

What does seem evident, whether it be the more radical scenario of Hargreaves or the more flexible application of the National Curriculum across all age ranges, is that diversity of provision is set to increase.

Developing a learning community rather than a school

Barber's (1996) 'Pupil Learning Resource Credit' and the 'Individual Learning Promise' can be seen as an attempt to bring back the responsibilities as well as the rights of parents. The framework that needs to be created is one in which there is a learning community responsible for children, rather than a community which passes all responsibility to the school. Indeed, the flaw in the school improvement and school effectiveness movements is that both see educational improvement solely through the school route. The 1997 White Paper, *Excellence in Schools* (DFEE), contained many of the government's ideas about the involvement of the wider community in the education of pupils.

The rationale for a clear shift to the *learning* process is also proposed by Barber (1996) in a section which he entitles 'The Limits of School Improvement, the Potential of Reengineering'. In a critique of the school improvement movement he comments:

> The question is, however, whether this focus on school improvement, though a necessary step forward, will ever be sufficient. In my view it is deficient as a model of educational salvation in four respects. Firstly, even in improving schools, there are sufficient numbers of pupils who slip through the net of educational success. Secondly, though many improving schools work hard at relations with parents, the focus on *school* improvement casts the parents in the role of (perhaps supportive, perhaps not) bystander.... Thirdly, the implicit assumption behind school improvement is that the aspirations of every learner can be met within one school ... this assumption becomes increasingly questionable and perhaps even absurd. Fourthly, the school-improvement movement, with its important focus on making schools responsible, also fails to address sufficiently the overall inadequacy of British cultural attitudes to education and learning.
>
> (Barber 1996: 247–248)

This is a clear rallying call to rethink the role of schools. Instead of being the sole providers they should be part of a wider learning network of providers and opportunities with shared responsibility for pupil achievement. The school can be at one of the pivotal points of this learning network but developing individual and community responsibility for education is as important as all the current attempts to reform schools to be more effective than they are (which could still make them fairly ineffective anyway!). Giving all post-16 pupils a learning voucher or credit for 'x' number of years education or 'x' amount of resources to be used in a personal learning plan may be a more effective way of seeing education as a process to be utilised instead of seeing it in terms of school attendance.

How teachers facilitate a learning day

If the traditional school year is under threat, then the traditional school day is even more threatened. The traditional school day is part of a factory model of schooling which sees the mass knowledge transfer system as the best way of achieving universal literacy. New conceptualisations of the school day are necessary now that we have greater expectations of the education system and the responsibility for learning can be seen to be switching from the teacher to the pupil. Indeed the expression 'school day' is itself becoming redundant.

In designing a 'learning day', the concept of self-management should apply to the pupil as well as to the institution. How do we encourage and support the pupils to become responsible for directing and organising their own learning? An appropriate model can be achieved by switching the emphasis to one in which the learner organises a series of learning experiences which, while they may focus around the school day, are not solely constrained within it. A package of activities that the learner assembles to meet her or his individual learning needs might include, in addition to school attendance, a combination of work on technology-based activity outside the school and attendance at a homework support centre. Barber (1996) talks of an 'Individual Learning Promise' where a 'Pupil Learning Resource Credit' is used to provide educational resources at home in order to reengineer learning resources to be focused on the child and not on the institution of the school. In this context, teachers are helping to organise a school day that fits into an overall learning day. As such they are not just delivering the immediate lesson but are consultants on the most appropriate learning strategy for the individual pupil to employ in a variety of learning situations. The most appropriate strategy might be teaching a concept to a whole group, although the group may be less homogeneous than heretofore.

Staff skills and competencies

The role of the teacher and the skills and competencies that they display will have to be rethought over the next few years as they meet the challenge of reengineered schools. Organising a learning programme and being the consultant on differentiated learning seems rather passive. We would not use concepts such as the teacher becoming a facilitator but regard him/her as being the 'wise' person who has the broader view and depth of knowledge not only to deliver part of the portfolio, but also to take on the role of 'Director of Studies' for each child. It is important to consider that while the technical competency to undertake a specific task is important, of greater significance are the generic competencies that individuals bring to a variety of situations. In teaching, while competence in a specific subject will remain important, a range of generic skills will take on increasing importance. Examples of these skills are: information retrieval; motivating students to work in self-directing learning groups; encouraging self-discipline so that learners take responsibility for their own work. Also, with the increase in the volume of information and the variety of information sources, an important range of skills will be the information ones. People will need to work in and manage staff teams in order to utilise these resources instead of being isolated teachers. Rethinking by individuals of their roles as teachers also necessitates a readiness to change and encompass new developments. We would consider, in simplistic but nevertheless valuable terms, that half of the challenge of coping with change is a resource problem and the other half is about reengineering 'mindsets'. The latter is probably more difficult to achieve! The McBer competencies of analytical and conceptual thinking allied to the 'flexibility' competency may be the ones which we need to develop as teachers rethink and regroup to meet the challenge of operating in this new environment (see Davies and Ellison 1997: 48).

Resourcing education

The twin constraints of limited or nil real growth in public expenditure and a commitment not to raise the basic rate of taxation mean that significant improvements in the quality of education are required without significant increases in public expenditure. Instead, different strategies will have to be used either to redeploy existing resources in different ways or to seek new and different sources of finance. Barber's (1996) suggestion of the 'Pupil Learning Resource Credit' being funded through taxing child benefit is one redistribution strategy. Perhaps more radical partnership models are appropriate, for example, the use of private finance as LEAs lease property or as funds are raised through the Private Finance Initiative (PFI). In the USA, after a hesitant start, the 'Whittle' schools (organised and run by the Whittle Corporation) have shown how private finance can be harnessed to public provision. They are contracted to the local school boards to provide education. In the UK, we have aided schools which receive 85 per cent of their capital and maintenance funding and 100 per cent of their revenue funding from the state while the remaining 15 per cent comes via the relevant religious group. So we already have a precedent for mixed funding of education. It should be possible, especially at the primary level, to encourage parents to set up their own schools with varying degrees of state and individual funding. This would allow for the development of schools which could more closely meet parental needs. Even private schools have never been 'truly' private. They receive differing degrees of state support in the form of charitable status, VAT (value-added tax) relief, graduate teachers from the state higher education system and the ability of private sector teachers to belong to the state's teachers' superannuation scheme. State support can thus be considered to be a matter of degree, rather than a simple either/or situation. Walden (1996) argues for the opening up of the private sector but perhaps what is needed is a more radical mixed private/state funding mechanism. The challenge of reengineering is to find better ways of using existing resources but also to find a means of harnessing both public and private finance in the search for educational improvement. The Education Action Zones (EAZs) are an interesting development here.

Equity issues

The moral question facing leaders in schools is how to give all the pupils in the school the best possible chance to fulfil their potential. Is it possible, if we offer differing provision to different groups, to ensure that they all have a fair share? Is it possible that if we can only benefit some pupils that we should do so, even though we know that it is impossible in the short-term to benefit everyone? Take the stereotypical 'leafy suburb' where resource levels at home mean that pupils not only receive their five or six hours of tuition in school but can have another five or six hours uninterrupted Internet or other technology-based support on their own computer at home. If we take a failing school (as identified by the Government) in a deprived inner city area, not only is the five or six hours of school-based learning inadequate, but pupils are unlikely to have the additional technology support at home. A double educational negative! Consider the scenario which follows.

A new headteacher is appointed to a school and decides not only on a plan to improve the teaching and learning but also to attack the technology gap. To do this she obtains sponsorship to buy some multi-media computers and to pay for staffing by IT experts. She charges all the pupils attending after school £1 for the session. She knows that not all the pupils can come – so she benefits the motivated and the ones able to pay rather than the unmotivated and those with limited funds. Progress in provision in the future is likely to come through such initiatives where there is benefit to some pupils but not all. Is that fair? Is any gain worth it?

These types of discussions are likely to occupy us as we move forward on diverse fronts at differing rates as the monolithic 'one size fits all' culture is replaced by individual initiatives and diversity of provision. This is a very simple example of how changes throw up major equity issues. Far more fundamental equity issues are brought to our attention by Hargreaves' (1997) analysis of the four types of school, especially the 'custodial school'. One of the key functions of the leader in this rapidly changing environment is to reassess and articulate the values which guide and underpin the school so that actions are consonant with these.

Ten trends – conclusion

These ten trends are possible developments that educational leaders should seek to understand but, more importantly, the leader and the school should build into their planning the appropriate structures and processes to develop the capability for what the surfers call 'looking outside'. This involves the surfer looking to the horizon, searching the small or medium waves for the one or two significant waves that it is worth riding. 'Looking outside' in education involves monitoring the trends and developments to pick out the significant ones. It is then worth spending time exploring these trends and building the organisational capability to understand them. This understanding is utilised as the school moves on to the next stage, that of building strategic intent (see Chapter 4). In the final section of this chapter, we give some ideas about how schools might undertake the first stage of establishing a futures perspective.

Building a futures perspective

Critics of futures thinking tend to rely on simplistic assertions that precise and detailed planning is not possible. That is certainly true. However, what is possible is to build a futures perspective in the school. This allows the school to build capability to understand trends and developments, to scan the environment and, most importantly, to build understanding of the nature of the trends as they develop.

While focusing on basic questions such as 'Why do we do what we do?', 'Does what we do contribute significant added value to the educational product?' and 'What do learners really need?' can be very valuable and important and can start the reengineering process, it is necessary to engage in 'planning backwards' by answering two basic questions:

- What sort of educational experience will learners need over the next ten years and beyond?
- How will we plan to operate in this environment?

How can a school move forward? We suggest two approaches based on establishing a futures group in a school.

Setting up a futures group in a school

A futures group can consist of a group of people who meet at approximately two-monthly intervals to consider the impact of possible futures on the school. This group can take a number of forms. It could be the traditional senior management team taking 'time out' to stand back and interpret what is happening in the wider environment. It could consist of a mixture of that group and governors who will represent a broader cross-section of experience. It may be more appropriate simply to have a cross-section of staff. In some areas, some headteachers meet with other heads on a termly basis for this purpose. Whatever grouping is chosen, it is important that the activity does not become a simple 'talking shop' but that some structure and coherence should be attempted. In particular it is important that key issues are identified and that the analysis progresses through data collection to scenario building.

This can be achieved in either of two ways as shown in Exercises 3.1 and 3.2.

Exercise 3.1: futures brainstorming

In this approach, the group starts with a 'clean slate' and engages in brainstorming about the future, having an unstructured discussion which then can be formalised, perhaps using the framework shown in Table 3.1.

Whilst carrying out this activity, it is important to look not just at the school sector but at the wider economic and social trends and to be creative by looking at a range of organisations and policies such as the information technology industry, the impact of the emerging economies, political and societal changes and their impact on the nature of work. The possible broader impact on the education sector can then be assessed.

Table 3.1 Brainstorming the future

Area for consideration	Evidence of trends/directions	Possible implications for education

A more structured approach than the one suggested in Exercise 3.1 would be to start with some pre-determined futures list. We suggest that schools take our ten reengineering trends as a start and, after discussion, identify five areas which they wish to monitor. Then, two or three times a year, they can undertake to report any significant developments or any items that urgently need adding to the list of five.

Exercise 3.2: reengineering trends

Choose five of the ten school reengineering trends outlined on pages 29 to 41 which your school should examine over the next 12 to 24 months. The aim should be to build in staff and governors the capability to understand the implications of these trends for the school. Choose those about which you, as a group, have little awareness, have not looked at recently or which might be particularly significant for your school. The focusing should allow the school to use its time effectively.

Consider the possible impact on the school of each of these and then suggest how the school might respond in order to cope with that impact. Record the results using the format in Table 3.2.

Table 3.2 Reengineering trends

Reengineering trends	Potential impact on the school	School response
I.		
2.		
3.		
4.		
5.		

This chapter has sought to build a futures perspective and to emphasise the need for a group in the school to engage in this long-term scanning. In the more intermediate future, strategy, strategic intent and strategic planning need to be employed. These concepts will be explored in the next chapter.

References

Barber, M. (1996) *The Learning Game*, London: Golancz.

Beare, H. and Slaughter, R. (1993) *Education for the Twenty First Century*, London: Routledge.

Caldwell, B. J. and Hayward, D. K. (1998) *The Future of Schools – Lessons from the Reform of Public Education*, London: Falmer Press.

Cannon, T. (1996) *Welcome to the Revolution: Managing Paradox in the Twenty-first Century*, London: Pitman.

Carr, D. K. and Johansson, H. J., (1995) *Best Practice Reengineering*, New York: McGraw-Hill.

Davies, B. (1997) 'Rethinking the educational context: a reengineering approach' in B. Davies and L. Ellison (1997) *School Leadership for the 21st Century: A Competency and Knowledge Approach*, London: Routledge.

Dent, H. S. (1995) *Jobshock*, New York: St Martin's Press.

Dettman, P. (1997) 'The laptop revolution' in B. Davies and J. West-Burnham (eds), *Reengineering and Total Quality in Schools*, London: Pitman.

DFEE (1997) *Excellence in Schools*, London: HMSO.

Drucker, P. (1993) *Post-capitalist Society*, New York: Harper Business.

Gates, B. (1995) *The Road Ahead*, New York: Penguin.

Guardian (1997) 'Three into five won't go' in *Guardian Education* 24/6/97 Schools 3.

Hammer, M. and Champy, J. (1993) *Reengineering the Corporation*, New York: HarperCollins.

Hammer, M. and Stanton, S. A. (1995) *The Reengineering Revolution: A Handbook*, New York: Harper Business.

Handy, C. (1994) *The Empty Raincoat: Making Sense of the Future*, London: Hutchinson.

Hargreaves, D. (1997) 'A Road to the Learning Society' in *School Leadership and Management* Vol. 17 No. 1: 9–21.

Lewis, J. (1997) 'From a blank sheet of paper' in B. Davies and J. West-Burnham (eds), *Reengineering and Total Quality in Schools*, London, Pitman.

Ohmae, K. (1995) *The End of the Nation State: The Rise of Regional Economies*, London: HarperCollins.

Naisbitt, J. (1996) *Megatrends Asia*, London: Nicholas Brealey.

Reich, R. (1992) *The Work of Nations*, New York: Vintage Books.

Southorn, N. (1997) 'Reengineering post-16 courses' in B. Davies and J. West-Burnham (eds), *Reengineering and Total Quality in Schools*, London: Pitman.

Walden, G. (1996) *We should know better: Solving the Education Problem*, London: Fourth Estate.

Chapter 4

Understanding strategy: strategic planning and strategic intent

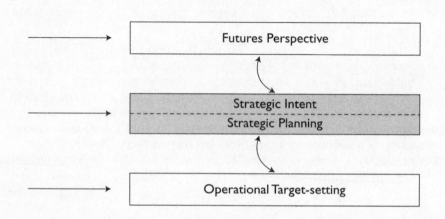

We hope that Chapter 3 has given school leaders the impetus and ideas to build a futures perspective. Once this outward and forward-looking mindset has been established, it will be necessary to seek ways in which the school might move on in order to prepare both the school and the pupils for the future. This requires that the school develops a strategy, which Johnson and Scholes (1997: 10) define as:

> the direction and scope of the organisation over the long term: which achieves advantage for the organisation through its config-uration of resources within a changing environment, to meet the needs of markets and to fulfil stakeholder expectations.

Quinn gives a similar definition of strategy to that of Johnson and Scholes. He sees it as being

> the pattern or plan that integrates an organisation's major goals, policies and action sequences into a cohesive whole. A well-formulated strategy helps to marshal and allocate an organisation's

resources into a unique and viable posture based on its relative internal competencies and shortcomings, anticipated changes in the environment, and contingent moves by intelligent opponents.

(Mintzberg, Ghoshal and Quinn 1995: 5)

In order to develop a strategy, Quinn sees the organisation as needing goals or objectives, policies, programmes and strategic decisions. This idea of strategy being seen as a complex concept is taken up, later in the same chapter, by Mintzberg who analyses the functions of strategy and provides us with what he calls the 'five P's for strategy':

1   Strategy as a *plan* – incorporating a consciously intended course of action, thus strategies are made in advance and are consciously taken.
2   Strategy as a *ploy* – such as taking a position to outwit an opponent.
3   Strategy as a *pattern* – by this definition strategy is consistency in behaviour. However, it is possible to distinguish between intended strategy where deliberate actions are taken and emergent strategy where patterns develop in the absence of intent or despite it.
4   Strategy as *position* – a means whereby the organisation orientates itself to a specific location in its market or field.
5   Strategy as *perspective* – a way of perceiving the world. A shared way in the organisation of looking at its role and position.

(Mintzberg, Ghoshal and Quinn 1995: 13–19)

These five Ps can be seen to be coming from a competitive environment, drawn from both the military and business roots of strategy. In this general usage, strategy can be seen to encompass the direction-setting for the longer term (say five years), working forward from today's operational base. It is clear that some idea of the organisation's direction and major activities is essential if it is to continue to be effective within its resource base.

Some of these concepts are more directly transferable to an educational setting than others. The problem in education is that there is a feeling of being unable to control what is happening because of externally imposed changes but this is, perhaps, an over-used excuse for not developing appropriate strategies for the circumstances. Some schools already have a strategic plan in order to realise their intended strategy. They see this plan as a rational proposal that rolls out over a three- to five-year period. Other schools have not gone down this route, believing that the pace of change is so great and so unpredictable that such plans are overtaken; these schools simply create a new one- to two-year plan each year. We believe that some aspects of a school's activities are quite predictable or determinable while other aspects are less so. We try, in this chapter, to develop approaches to meet these two different requirements. We discuss strategic planning as being appropriate for the 'determinable' aspects of medium-term planning. We then consider what can be done to overcome the difficulties of planning forward in a rapidly changing environment. We propose the concept of strategic intent which we believe is a more appropriate way of signposting the future of the school for the less predictable aspects of provision.

Strategic planning

We now focus on one specific aspect of strategy development and a process which schools are being encouraged to use to create three- or five-year plans, that of strategic planning for an intended course of action. In an earlier work (Davies and Ellison 1997: 81) we defined strategic planning as 'the systematic analysis of the school and its environment and the formulation of a set of key strategic objectives to enable the school to realise its vision, within the context of its values and its resource potential'.

Strategic planning takes up a number of the themes outlined above by Mintzberg, Ghoshal and Quinn (1995). It involves journey thinking in which we are extrapolating patterns from the past and projecting to the future. It takes the broader organisational view. It projects forward several years. It articulates the main features of the organisation's development. As such it can be considered to be both a rational and, to a large degree, an incremental process.

What would a strategic plan look like in a school? We suggest it would have a number of key features. Instead of being the traditional school development plan list of tasks to be done it would aggregate these numerous activities into a limited number of strategic areas. The example, in Table 4.1, shows how the core purpose of the school, *the learning outcomes* is the first strategic planning area followed by the *support for the quality of the learning and teaching processes* to achieve this and, finally, by the third area which comprises a number of *management arrangements* that underpin the activities above. The strategic planning activities which are undertaken are definable and achievable within a given time frame and the person responsible for seeing that they are achieved is listed, together with associated costs. In Chapter 6 we show a fully worked out grid by using a case example of the strategic activities needed to secure the raising of achievement in terms of increasing the overall success rate in external assessments. The important factor in this process is for the leader in the school to focus on aggregated strategic data and activities and not to become involved in the detail of the operational target-setting process. Therefore, the plan is shown in broad strategic areas.

Table 4.1 A strategic planning framework

Strategic Planning Area	Strategic Planning Activities	Time Frame	Responsibility	Cost
The learning outcomes: pupil progress & achievement				
Support for the quality of learning & teaching processes				
Management arrangements: physical & financial resources, school structure & organisation				

In our experience, many people in a wide range of schools have found this to be a format which is easy to understand and which is systematic. It has the benefit of focusing activities around a set of major strategic activities and, by so doing, provides a clear agenda for the school. The successful use of strategic planning is based on there being a predictable environment which can be identified so that appropriate strategies can be implemented in a rational, steady way. Our concern is whether the outcome of the strategic planning process, i.e. the medium- to long-term, clearly defined plan is appropriate for all of a schools' activities, a point which we will discuss next.

Problems of strategic planning processes

Strategic planning may well be useful for the more predictable and controllable elements within the planning processes, especially when these are incremental and linear and where a good understanding of the detail is possible. We contend, however, that there are problems associated with this approach, particularly in an era of rapid change. It assumes a rational and predictable process which, in practical terms, may not be possible in a turbulent, dynamic environment such as we have now. It may also tend to be very incremental, which leads to the danger that instead of taking a fresh zero-based view of the planning needs of the next five years, the present plan and its associated culture lead to a focus on adjustments and developments rather than on a fundamental review of core activities. Thus, strategic planning and development obscure or overtake the need for more radical strategic rethinking. As far back as 1987, Porter was perceptive in his observation that there was: 'a growing recognition that the processes for strategic planning were not promoting strategic thinking ... meaningless long-term projections obscured strategic insight' (Porter 1987: 22). Similarly, Hamel and Prahalad provided an analysis of the problems of strategy formulation and strategic planning in the Harvard Business Review in 1989. They saw strategy as incorrectly being utilised as a marginal adjustment approach:

> We believe that the application of the concepts such as 'strategic fit' (between resources and opportunities), 'generic strategies', (low cost vs. differentiation vs. focus) and the strategy hierarchy (goals, strategies, and tactics) have often abetted the process of competitive decline ... marginal adjustments to current orthodoxies are no more likely to produce competitive revitalisation than are marginal improvements in operating efficiency.
>
> (Hamel and Prahalad 1989: 63)

In a continuing attack on the limitations of strategic planning, Hamel and Prahalad make a number of statements which challenge current approaches such as 'strategic plans reveal more about today's problems than tomorrow's opportunities' (p. 66) and 'the predictive horizon is becoming shorter and shorter. So plans do little more than project the present forward incrementally' (p. 66).

In a perceptive critique, they put forward the view that two contrasting models of strategy have emerged. One, allied to traditional models of strategic planning, concerns maintaining 'strategic fit' where the emphasis is on 'trimming ambitions to match available resources' (p. 65). The other model is concerned with the problem of 'leveraging resources to reach seemingly unattainable goals' (p. 65). While the first maintains consistency in adherence to financial goals, the second is achieved by allegiance to a particular strategic intent. It is this second goal which reflects the current demands of the education service. Schools (and, indeed other sectors of education) are being forced to consider new ways of operating rather than blaming their lack of effectiveness on limited resource availability.

These problems of strategic planning can also be seen to apply to the environment in which many schools find themselves. As a useful exercise, the reader can undertake a case study of his/her own school and articulate the problems that have been experienced over the last year in the school in attempting to undertake strategic planning activities to create a three- to five-year plan.

Exercise 4.1 Problems of strategic planning

List the problems that you have encountered in undertaking the strategic planning process in your school.

We now move on to consider other approaches which may be more appropriate for certain parts of a school's medium-term planning.

Alternative planning perspectives and approaches

Boisot (1995) examines strategy and suggests that control, which is inherent in the concept of strategy, is rendered ineffective because of the turbulence caused by rapidly increasing rates of change. As a result he identifies four basic types of response: strategic planning, emergent strategy, intrapreneurship and strategic intent and links them with this turbulence and with levels of understanding. In Figure 4.1 the vertical axis relates to the degree of turbulence and, hence, change in the environment

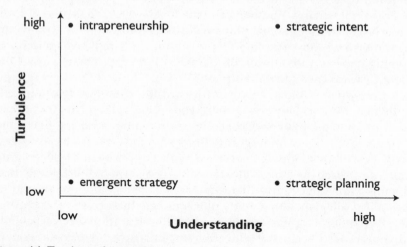

Figure 4.1 Typology of strategies.
Source: Boisot 1995: 40.

and the horizontal axis relates to the level of understanding that an organisation has of the turbulence and change in which it exists.

For *strategic planning* to be successful, the rate of change is assumed to be less than the organisation's ability to understand and adapt to that change. In such a case, the fact that activities can be planned, implemented and the results evaluated in a reasonably consistent and proactive manner is due to one of two factors. First, the environment is one which is shorter-term and therefore more predictable or, second, the nature of the activity is incremental and not subject to significant turbulence or change. Thus, a school in such a situation can have a clear strategic plan for the definable part of its activities. In the educational context, rapid change over the last ten years and the future impact of technology on learning have cast doubts as to whether strategic planning over a three- to five-year period is possible for all of a school's activities. Schools have been encouraged to extend their development planning period from one or two years up to five years and have tried to make plans for this less predicable environment. Whether it is practicable to do this remains in some doubt. Boisot (1995: 33–35) suggests that alternative approaches should be considered.

Emergent strategy assumes that there will be incremental change with adjustments made to the planned strategy as new information becomes available. Planners assume that a process of 'disjointed incrementalism' will change their plans as they go along. This approach is commonly found in organisations which exist in stable environments but where there are fairly low levels of management understanding. Thus the organisation can respond and adjust as each new change 'hits' them. Schools, when faced with a series of new initiatives from central or local government, react and adjust to them as they come along without seeing the pattern or purpose of what is happening. This is typical of reactive, as against proactive, organisations. Similarly, within schools, various groups react and respond to instructions from the school leadership without understanding the intent or overall purposes of the organisation.

Intrapreneurship assumes that there is a high degree of turbulence in the system and that the centre of the organisation does not have the understanding to plan in an integrated way. As a result, decentralised units are encouraged to react to their specific circumstances and to relate to the centre in a loosely coupled way. Thus, localised successes and failures build a direction for the organisation. This can be seen to have operated in education at a number of levels. For the education sector as a whole, the multiple initiatives of the 1980s were imposed upon schools at the same time that they were given greater autonomy at the site level to manage their responses. As such, it could be considered that the national government had little or no understanding (did it care?) as to how the implementation would be accomplished but merely held the sub-units (the LEAs or the schools) accountable. Similarly, the head-teacher of a large secondary or primary school, faced with the then new National Curriculum over the full range of subjects could not hope individually to plan a detailed response. With a high volume of change over such a range of subjects and the inability to understand the detail of each, the only sensible response was to let the individual curri-culum leaders develop their own understanding and response. Only later, when the pace of curricular change had slowed was it possible for the leader in the school to comprehend fully the nature of the change over such a wide range of fronts and for other planning strategies to become available. Thus, intrapreneurship is not a good or bad strategy, but it can be an appropriate strategy in a given set of circumstances.

Strategic intent, the final approach, is one which has a great deal of value for the educationalist, as an alternative to strategic planning. Intent is about setting a series of achievable but significantly difficult activities that 'leverage up' the organisation to perform at much higher levels in specific and definable areas. Thus, developing a 'success culture' as against a 5 per cent increase in pass rates can be seen to be an example that delineates an intent from a specific plan. Another example would be to develop a culture of independent technology-based learning in the school. Strategic intent is a very powerful way of linking futures thinking and strategy as a means of providing direction and purpose for an organisation, whereas broad visions or goals may be too vague to be of practical use to the school. We will now 'unpack' the concept of strategic intent a little further.

Developing strategic intent in schools

Strategic intent is described by Boisot (1995: 36) as 'a process of coping with turbulence through a direct, intuitive understanding, emanating from the top of the firm and guiding its efforts'. We would suggest that a school which is dealing with either a longer-term time frame or a less predictable environment needs to build in all of its staff a common strategic intent, based on the values and ambitions of the school, which all staff can articulate and to which they can align themselves. Thus, faced with new and untried situations they can draw on that common understanding as a frame of reference.

To further our understanding of strategic intent we build on Boisot's work by adding perspectives from the work of Hamel and Prahalad (1989: 64) who see that:

> strategic intent envisions a desired leadership position and establishes the criterion the organisation will use to chart its progress.... The concept also encompasses an active management process that includes: focusing the organisation's attention ... motivating people by communicating the value of the target; leaving room for individual and team contributions; sustaining enthusiasm by providing new operational definitions as circumstances change; and using intent consistently to guide resource allocations.

Earlier in the chapter we quoted Hamel and Prahalad on strategic intent, in relation to the 'leveraging of resources to reach seemingly unattainable goals'. (1989: 65). This positive approach fits with their view of the key characteristics and advantages of strategic intent as:

- Strategic intent is stable over time
- Strategic intent provides consistency to short-term action, while leaving room for reinterpretation as new opportunities emerge
- Strategic intent sets a target that deserves personal effort and commitment

(Hamel and Prahalad 1989: 63)

The value of this approach is that it involves a considerable 'stretch' for an organisation as it is *setting key areas of achievement where precise articulation of detail is not possible*. It forces the organisation to be imaginative and inventive in seeking new ways to create capability and to achieve its goals. Intent does not involve every single aspect of the school's activity. Many tasks and activities that are of an incremental and linear nature will be undertaken through the strategic planning process. However, many key fundamental or radical developments will not fit into this incremental process. This is where strategic intent comes into its own. A school will need to establish key areas of intent that will focus attention and enable it to build capability in those areas so that the journey of reaching them will 'flesh out' the detail. In order to demonstrate what we mean by strategic intent, we now show strategic intents for a school and for a school system.

Example one: Brentwich School

Brentwich School, after undertaking a 'futures awareness' training session and an extensive strategic analysis (see chapter 5), decided to focus on building capability to deal with five key intents by the leadership and staff.

Table 4.2 Strategic intents for the school

1. Create a high expectation and success culture
2. Design and implement accurate performance indicators and hold everyone accountable for them
3. Establish technology-based individual learning for all pupils
4. Build 'leadership in-depth' throughout the staff
5. Link home and school through the development of a learning community

Example two: Children Achieving: a school reform agenda in Philadelphia

The *Children Achieving* reform is organised around ten components which chart a five-year course of educational reform (see Appendix for full details). It seeks to build capability in the schools around ten strategic intents rather than starting with a prescriptive and detailed plan. These are shown in Table 4.3.

These challenging intents are seen as a framework and capability-building agenda for the schools to work through. The outcome in detailed

Table 4.3 Strategic intents for Children Achieving

1. Set high expectations for everyone
2. Design accurate performance indicators to hold everyone accountable for results
3. Shrink the centralised bureaucracy and let schools make more decisions
4. Provide intensive and sustained professional development to all staff
5. Make sure that all students are ready for schools
6. Provide students with the community support and services they need to succeed in school
7. Provide up-to-date technology and institutional materials
8. Engage the public in shaping, understanding, supporting and participating in school reform
9. Ensure adequate resources and use them effectively
10. Be prepared to address all of these priorities together and for the long-term – starting now

terms and the means of achieving it will be worked out during the five-year time-frame.

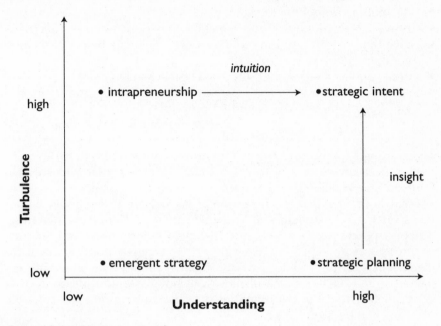

Figure 4.2 Intuition versus insight.
Source: Boisot 1995: 42.

Boisot (1995: 41) sees strategic intent as developing either from 'insight' gained through the strategic planning process or from 'intuition' gained through the intrapreneurial process (see Figure 4.2). This brings into play the leadership competencies and skills of judgement and intuition based on insights rather than utilising a simple linear rational approach. As such it may offer a more appropriate decision-making context in today's turbulent educational environment.

Achieving a specific strategic intent involves significant creativity with respect to means. Most importantly, it provides a framework and a set of goals for those inside the school to measure their contribution. This also presents problems, however, as it can create tensions because there is inevitably a mismatch between the current resource base and set of activities and the articulated set of strategic intents. It is also the case that no one has a precise map of what the intent will look like in five years' time, so the senior leadership in the school has to give a great deal of attention to managing the journey. As such strategic intent sets a series of challenges which are followed by a succeeding set of challenges. By definition, leadership is more prescriptive about ends and very flexible about the means to those ends. Hamel and Prahalad see that, in managing this process, leaders need to:

- create a sense of urgency
- develop a competitor focus
- provide the employees with the skills they need to work effectively
- give the organisation time to digest one challenge before launching another
- establish clear milestones and review mechanisms
- see the need for reciprocal responsibility – sharing the 'pain and gain' between employers and employees

(Hamel and Prahalad 1989: 67–68)

These are very significant features of an effective organisation. Some of them reflect key aspects of the National Standards for Headteachers in England and Wales.

What does all this mean for schools? We believe that schools should focus on the two domains of strategic intent and strategic planning. Schools operate partly in a highly turbulent environment and, in such circumstances, the appropriate strategy is to create a strategic intent for the school. Part of a school's environment is more predictable and less turbulent and, in those circumstances, techniques and approaches that are available from the traditional business school approach to strategic planning can be useful.

With strategic intent, the school can be seen (as in Figure 4.3) to move upward and to the right as it establishes a process of coping with turbulence by understanding broad major intents and 'binding' people to them by establishing them as core purposes of the organisation. As

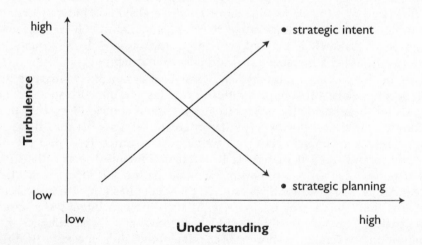

Figure 4.3 Strategic intent and strategic planning.
Source: Boisot 1995: 40.

such it does not concern itself with the detail of strategic planning but organises commitment around these key intents. At a later stage, when the school has developed its capability in a particular area, it will then either be able to operationalise the activities through creating a detailed plan *or* it will have to reformulate the intent, once a clearer understanding of the dimensions of the area have been established, in order to build further capability.

With strategic planning, the school is trying to reduce the turbulence through greater knowledge and understanding. As it does this and increases its level of understanding it moves down from left to right in (Figure 4.3) and is able to plan more and more of its activities.

In order to build strategic intent or to create more specific strategic plans, it is necessary to have an information base from which to operate. Part of the longer-term picture will have been established from the consideration of a 'futures' perspective in Chapter 3 but this can be supplemented significantly through using well-established approaches from within the strategic analysis literature. To achieve this we move on, in Chapter 5, to the gathering and interpretation of data to inform the school's process of creating a strategic intent and a strategic plan.

References

Boisot, M. (1995) 'Preparing for turbulence' in B. Garratt (ed.) *Developing Strategic Thought*, London: McGraw-Hill.

Davies, B. and Ellison, L.(1997) *School Leadership for the 21st Century: A Competency and Knowledge Approach*, London: Routledge.

Hamel, G. and Prahalad, C. K. (1989) 'Strategic Intent' *Harvard Business Review*, May/June: 63–76.

Johnson, G. and Scholes, K. (1997) *Exploring Corporate Strategy*, 4th edn, London: Prentice Hall.

Mintzberg, H., Ghoshal, S. and Quinn, J .B. (1995) *The Strategy Process* (Euro. edn), Hemel Hempstead: Prentice Hall.

Porter, M. (1987) 'Corporate Strategy: The State of Strategic Thinking' *The Economist*, May 23.

Chapter 5

Strategic analysis

Obtaining the data and building a
strategic view

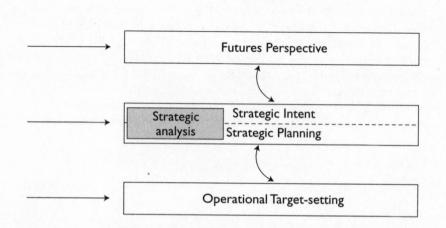

Strategic analysis aims to form a view of the key factors which will influence the school in the medium-term. These factors will affect the strategies which are chosen to achieve the strategic intent and the strategic plan. Strategic analysis can be seen in practical terms to involve two sequential processes: first obtaining strategic data and, second, building an aggregated strategic view of the school through interpreting and integrating that data to turn it into useful information.

Obtaining strategic data

What sort of area or activities should be part of the strategic analysis? In Table 5.1 we put forward a taxonomy of four areas for analysis and indicate the corresponding information needed and some of the approaches available for collecting the data.

Although the information will usually be assembled by the senior management team, to appreciate fully the strategic position of the school it is necessary to understand how a wide range of stakeholders, such as pupils, staff, employers, governors and the community, view the situation which the school faces and its possible direction. Those responsible for aspects of the analysis need to look beyond their normal sources of information if the work is to have validity.

The sections which follow take the reader through the four areas in Table 5.1.

Table 5.1 Taxonomy of strategic data collection

Area for analysis	Data needed	Available approaches
The environment	international trends national trends regional/local trends	PESTLE analysis (political, economic, socio-cultural, technological, legal, educational)
The school's customers or stakeholders	existing and potential customers or clients	market segmentation demographic and survey data
	their values, wants and needs	preference surveys
The school's product and service	areas of strength and weakness, growth and contraction	SWOT analysis GRIDS
	perceptions of the school	internal evaluation external inspection attitude surveys
The competitors	the products and services offered, their strengths and weaknesses	SWOT analysis customer survey data
	perceptions of their provision	competitor analysis inspection reports

Analyse the environment

One of the most significant strategic roles for school leadership is 'managing the boundaries', that is seeing beyond the boundaries of the school and understanding the interface between the school and its environment. Those who engage constantly in futures thinking should be very aware of the global trends (see Chapter 3). Here we seek to remind people to consider those trends and thus to bring their implications into the broad planning process. We seek also to encourage schools to look to international comparisons, particularly within education and, closer to home, to gather data on what is happening or likely to be happening at national and local levels, both in education and more generally.

For the purposes of strategic analysis, the external environment can be sub-divided into international (or global), national (or macro) and regional/local (or micro). This categorisation affects the degree of detail which is available and, sometimes, the degree of its impact over time. There are many analytical frameworks which can be used (such as a PESTLE analysis which examines political, economic, socio-cultural, technological, legal and educational factors) in order to categorise the trends and to check that all areas have been covered. It is important to choose a framework which covers the relevant areas and which can be readily used by those in school without being too much of a drain on people's time.

The international environment

It seems probable that organisations (including schools) which survive and prosper will be those which have flexibility and can respond rapidly to change. The global trends should indicate some significant implications for schools such as:

- the technology of learning will change;
- learners and teachers in various locations will be brought closer together by communication systems;
- a very wide range of information will be quickly and cheaply accessible;
- pupils will need to be prepared for the world after school in which work will be varied, more internationally based and more often of a service rather than a production nature.

An understanding of this international environment will allow schools to offer a range of experiences to pupils and staff and to benchmark themselves against similar schools elsewhere.

The national environment

The PESTLE framework is a useful tool for identifying and classifying the national trends that will impact on schools and the learning process in the future. *Political* developments which can affect schools would include: the role of the public sector in general and in education in particular; policies on appropriate types of school; admissions policies. In the *economic* category, schools need to consider: national trends in employment, in terms of the percentage likely to be in work, the nature of that work, the pay and conditions patterns; the nature of the economy and the impact of European policy; trends in public expenditure; trends in educational funding such as relating it to outputs and mixing sources (private/public; state/parental top-up). *Socio-cultural* trends which might be identified could include the changing gender roles and a more mobile and multi-cultural society, the emphasis on lifelong learning and the involvement of the community in that learning.

Although it is difficult to keep pace with changes in *technology*, the global trends can be identified at the national level. These would include the ability to store, retrieve and transmit large amounts of information very quickly, the availability of technology in the home, the community and in education. In the UK, schools must consider trends in European *legislation* as well as that which might emerge nationally. Schools are affected by a constantly changing set of regulations and, while it is important that someone understands the detail, it is also important to be aware of trends, especially in relation to Health and Safety, opportunities to learn and employment law. Senior managers in schools are probably more aware of national trends in *education* than in other areas but there is still a tendency to concentrate on the present and to ignore future trends such as the possible outcome of major curriculum or assessment reviews. As a minimum, schools can consider the directions which are indicated by government publications and by the significant research projects such as those on school improvement.

The local environment

Schools are increasingly being affected by a variety of factors in the local or regional environment such as:

- the development of regional government and associated policies and projects;
- local government policies;
- industrial or rural regeneration projects;
- levels of employment/unemployment;
- housing developments;
- demographic trends;
- transport infrastructure;
- community expectations of local services;
- competitors in the provision of education;
- lifelong learning initiatives;
- the broadening of educational options at all stages.

Often it is not necessary to have precise information but, rather, a grasp of the significant trends. Local and regional bodies can usually supply any details which are required and often have graphs indicating trends. The school must consider whether or not such information is a prediction of the future or merely an extrapolation of the past.

Undertaking the environmental analysis

All staff need to have an awareness of the trends in the external environment and their likely impact on schools so that they can understand the reasoning behind various proposals at the school level and the need for flexibility and responsiveness. Groups may be formed and individuals named to keep an eye on trends at each level. Such groups could include governors, staff, parents and pupils and could meet, say, twice a year. The case example shown opposite demonstrates a possible outcome of this type of analysis, using the trends which were identified in Chapter 3.

Exercise 5.1: a PESTLE analysis of the environment

Either individually or as a group, fill in the significant changes that you consider are happening in each of the categories below.

	International	National	Local
Political			
Economic			
Socio-cultural			
Technological			
Legal			
Educational			

Case example 5.1: a PESTLE analysis at the national level

Political
- Significantly enhanced levels of consumer choice, reflected in the differentiation between schools and the ability to choose a school.
- Greater international co-operation.

Economic

- Relating value-added educational gains to resource levels, allowing schools to be compared in terms of 'value for money' and forcing them to achieve increased performance with the same resource level.
- Considerable changes in staffing patterns and arrangements, more para-professionals, core and periphery staff, fixed-term performance-led contracts, school-site pay bargaining.
- Greater varieties of finance with blurring between state-only and private-only funding of schools.
- Contracting-out of educational as well as service elements of schooling.

Socio-cultural

- A re-examination of the boundaries between different stages of education and between education and the community.
- A focus on the importance of learning.

Technological factors

- Radical changes in the nature of teaching and learning as the impact of the new teaching and learning technologies gathers pace.

Legal

- The increasing use of short-term contracts for staff.

Educational

- A focus on high achievement
- The development of centralised curriculum and testing frameworks which provide measures of output and value-added, thus increasing information for parental choice.
- Redefinition of the leadership and management functions in schools.

Analyse the school's customers or stakeholders

Here the purpose is to identify two main sets of strategic information:

- who are the customers or stakeholders and who might they be in the future? This can be achieved through market segmentation;
- what do the clients/customers want from the school? This information can be gathered in a variety of ways, for example through preference surveys.

There are several caveats to offer to those who may consider these approaches. Vast amounts of data may be gathered with considerable time implications. It is better to think carefully about the type of information which the school requires before asking a lot of people a lot of questions. Also, the responses, particularly to attitude surveys, can be very disturbing. There needs to be careful preparation in relation to planning the dissemination of results. It is unwise to gather data and then to take no action on issues that arise, although the action needed may simply be to improve communication.

Market segmentation

Market segmentation is used to divide diverse clients or stakeholders into more homogeneous groups in order to identify particular wants, needs and influencing factors. Appropriate products and services can then be developed and effective means of communication can be devised. A first step could be to divide the clients/customers into those internal and those external to the school. Once the segments have been identified, the school can then move on to examine a range of information such as numbers, gender, educational experience, preferences and attitudes.

When looking at *internal stakeholders*, it is important to consider the various groupings within the school so that any future direction is related to their varied needs. The most obvious categorisation would be into pupils and their parents, members of staff (teaching and support), governors, regular visitors and helpers. Within these categories, there are various sub-divisions, for example of pupils according to age, staff according to experience or function, governors according to areas of interest or influence and visitors according to affiliation and purpose.

There is a need to consider the wider *external stakeholders*, both individuals and groups, within and beyond the education system. These can include former and prospective pupils and their parents, prospective staff, the local community, commerce and industry, the Local Education

Authority and other educational institutions. In the wider context there would be national bodies such as the Teacher Training Agency, the General Teaching Council and the Office for Standards in Education (OFSTED).

Preference surveys

In countries which offer parents and pupils a choice of schools, the very survival of the school depends on taking account of their values and preferences (or wants). An awareness of preferences allows the school to develop appropriate activities and then to target those most likely to benefit. It avoids the school falling into the trap of 'producer capture' in which the deliverers determine the product without reference to the consumers. It is, however, important for educational leaders to avoid the reactive approach in which an over-emphasis is given to a wide spectrum of consumer demands so that the educational needs of children are not being met. Some customers/clients express wants strongly and may falsely influence the view of needs.

In its strategic analysis, the school must gather information on the *preferences (or wants)* of the various client groups. The information should then be used with care. It would not be possible or appropriate to react to all the preferences expressed. Some might result in the provision of ineffective education and others may be conflicting and cause confusion and inconsistencies within the school. If school leaders are fully informed about clients' preferences, they are then able to adjust provision if it is inappropriate or to communicate more effectively the existing provision.

When examining parental wants there should be an examination of current wants and future possible wants or preferences. This can be achieved by:

- interviews;
- focus groups;
- questionnaires;
- secondary data available locally or from national statistics and research projects.

Research by West (1992) showed that middle class parents who chose schools in a different LEA to their home did so because of their perceptions of discipline, good examination results and 'a pleasant atmosphere'. The research by Glatter, Woods and Bagley (1995) which covered a range of types of school, socio-economic circumstances and area demonstrated that parents have common priorities when choosing schools:

- child's preference for the school;
- standard of academic education;
- nearness to home/convenience for travel;
- child's happiness at the school.

The core business of the school is to meet the *needs* of the pupils so it is important to identify these clearly. The school must ensure that it has efficient ways of bringing together a wide range of data and information, much of it from school records, in order to:

- understand the socio-cultural background of the pupils;
- understand pupil potential;
- understand levels of attainment and learning difficulties prior to entry;
- identify appropriate learning strategies;
- maintain records of achievement and attainment throughout the time that a pupil is in school and monitor progress;
- keep up-to-date with national educational requirements, e.g. relating to curriculum and assessment;
- predict the future needs of the current pupils (e.g. through an understanding of environmental factors);
- predict the needs of future pupils;
- ensure that socialisation needs are kept under review.

In order to ensure that the school develops the capability to meet the pupil needs, there must be an analysis of the developmental requirements (for knowledge, skills and understanding) of the other internal clients such as the staff and governors.

Analyse the school's product and service

The product and service of a school needs to be analysed in its broadest sense. While much of the professional focus will be on the curriculum and assessment, those outside the school may make their judgements based on the effectiveness of communications, pupil behaviour and the possession by the pupils of basic and social skills. In planning an analysis of its product and service, all the school's provision should be listed, especially bearing in mind those areas which the clients feel are its significant activities. This would include:

- the formal curriculum;
- learning and teaching strategies used (in terms of range and effectiveness);

- measures of literacy, numeracy and cognitive ability;
- assessment and testing processes;
- ability and attainment levels on entry and exit;
- numbers with special educational needs;
- results from key stages and GCSE/A-level;
- calculations of value-added – over time, by individuals, teachers and pupils, by teams and in proportion to resources;
- extra-curricular activities;
- pupil discipline and appearance;
- relationships;
- resources levels and utilisation of resources – time, materials, hardware;
- staff skills and abilities in terms of learning and teaching skills and experience;
- perceptions of the pupil experience from the customer viewpoint;
- environment;
- ethos.

Various tools and techniques are available to analyse the situation in each area. The suitability of each will depend on a range of factors such as the time available, the people to be involved and the culture of the organisation.

SWOT analysis

This commonly used tool provides an analysis of the strengths and weaknesses of the school, the opportunities which are available and the threats which it faces, as perceived by a range of stakeholders. This is a quick and easy means of gathering information although it must be interpreted with care. The process is more fully developed in our book *Strategic Marketing for Schools* (Davies and Ellison 1997b). We also use the technique later in this chapter as a means of integrating and interpreting data.

Guidelines for Review and Internal Development in Schools (GRIDS)

This process provides a detailed and structured school-based review process which can be used to gain the involvement and commitment of staff (see Abbott *et al.* 1988).

Attitude surveys

These will enable the school to assess the perceptions which the existing and potential customers have of education in general and of the school in particular. If information gathered is to be valid, school leaders must give serious thought to the data collection process and to anonymity. We have been involved in different research projects in this area. In one, a group of schools wanted more information on the drift of pupils to another group of schools (see Davies and Ellison 1993). Another project involved us in working with each school to investigate the perceptions of a large number of pupils, their parents and all the staff (see Davies and Ellison 1997b).

Internal monitoring and evaluation

These processes would take place as part of the school's normal management cycle and would provide an ongoing source of information for the planning process. We explore these areas in more depth in the companion book to this one.

External inspection

All maintained schools in England and Wales have now been inspected by OFSTED and, in many cases, by others brought in to give an external perspective. The reports provide a wealth of data which can be built into the planning process. In the case of an OFSTED inspection, the school has to draw up an Action Plan and this will form an integral part of the school's normal planning process.

We feel that it is important to strike a cautionary note about the need to find out what the clients *really* think, rather than to make assumptions about their perceptions of the school's product and service. Also, these perceptions may not reflect the reality in the school but be the result of poor communication. Further investigation may be needed and a range of clients should be considered because different clients and client groups will have a different perception of the same aspect of provision.

Analyse the competitors

The information gathered about competitors and potential competitors can be very significant in determining the appropriate strategic direction of the school. As was suggested in Chapter 3, there are considerable issues here because of parental choice, developments in the learning technology and changes in the funding of education and in the continuum of education itself.

There is a tendency to see local schools as the competitors but the traditional product and service of the school can now, and increasingly will in the future, be offered by a range of other 'providers' such as

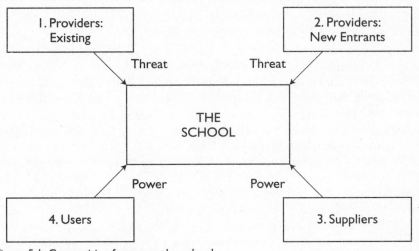

Figure 5.1 Competitive forces on the school.
Source: adapted from Davies and Ellison 1997b: 59

satellite, the World Wide Web, the National Grid for Learning, private agencies, industry and commerce, parents and the community. The conclusion to be drawn here is that any analysis of competitors must go far beyond the usual brief consideration of what 'the school down the road' is doing. Using concepts developed by Porter (1980) and Bowman and Asch (1987), we have developed a framework for analysing a school's competitors (see Figure 5.1). We believe that the existing and potential new providers of education can pose a threat to the school while the various stakeholders exercise power. It is important to analyse the nature of these threats and power relationships in order to be proactive in planning the school's response.

Each of the four areas will now be discussed.

Existing providers

It is important to analyse schools that are in the immediate environment as they exert power in the form of rivalry. Many schools need to look beyond the immediate area as rivals such as independent schools and those specialising in the performing arts draw from a wider catchment area. Also, benchmarking against schools in a wider national or international setting can provide a broader perception of what can be achieved and of potential competition. Good sources of information about other providers are: governors, parents, those who have chosen other schools, newspaper features, prospectuses, OFSTED reports and league tables.

New entrants

In the rapidly changing environment, schools as learning organisations are increasingly under threat as alternatives emerge from which pupils and their parents may choose. Sometimes these are new schools or developments of existing schools such as the move into a different age range. More often, in times of constrained resources for public expenditure and teacher recruitment problems, the competition comes from alternative forms of education. Home schooling becomes more feasible as information technology becomes more sophisticated and able to provide curriculum programmes, learning resources, links to other organisations and so on. It is useful for senior leaders in the school to consider the position from the new entrant's point of view, asking such questions as 'Why does the new entrant feel that there is a demand for the product or service?' or 'How does the new entrant perceive the existing providers?' Another interesting perspective is that of the pupils and parents: they often have very positive views, seeing a new provider as offering an exciting alternative.

Schools need to consider whether they can turn threats into opportunities by integrating the ideas into their own provision or whether they should compete based on other strengths. There is a need to think creatively and to look beyond education for trends which can be ascertained from the broader changes in the economy and technology.

Suppliers

Suppliers of goods or labour to the school can exert a powerful force so it is important to bear them in mind during strategic analysis. It may be that most of the factors are included elsewhere in the analysis but the following checklists need to be considered.

Suppliers of goods and services:

- Which are the main suppliers?
- Are the suppliers likely to be available in the future?
- What are the pricing and service level trends in each case?
- Is the school likely to be tied to the suppliers in any way, e.g. because of sponsorship deals, monopolies or legal requirements?

Suppliers of labour:

- Is there an adequate and appropriate supply from which to choose or should the school seek to improve the supply?
- How stable is the current labour supply?

- How much flexibility is there in the current labour supply?
- What are the cost implications of the current labour supply?

Analysis of the situation will allow the school to make appropriate plans or develop strategic intent to ensure that cost-effective supplies of goods and labour are available and that it is not driven by such powers.

Users

A school is mainly funded on a *per capita* basis so that an appropriate number of 'users' in the form of pupils or other funded learners is critical to its ability to remain cost-effective and 'in business'. Depending on the age of the pupils, it may be that the actual choice decision is significantly influenced by the parents. The factors which influence choice will have been considered in the section on preference surveys above. It might be useful to consider here the nature of the power which the users hold. If, for example, there are several ways of obtaining a similar type of education, then it is easy for users to change and they are quite powerful. Thus, issues such as a differentiated curriculum and a lack of geographical competitors weaken the power of the user. Conversely, a national curriculum, an effective transport system (or parents to act as 'chauffeurs') or a technology-based alternative strengthen the power of the user.

The users of the output of education i.e. other schools, the community and employers, exert power on schools. It is important to analyse their requirements in order to inform strategic developments.

Building an aggregated strategic view

Once all the information has been gathered together, it needs to be organised in some useful way in order to inform the choice of direction for the school. There are many ways in which this *integration* of information can be achieved. We describe below the use of five tools or models which we have chosen because they have proved useful to a variety of school leaders with whom we have worked:

1   Boston Consulting Group matrix
2   General Electric Screen
3   Macro SWOT
4   Kawasaki's matrix
5   Little's lifecycle portfolio matrix

Each of the models allows the school to build up a rounded picture which can promote discussion about developments. In order for the pattern built up to be valid, the planning team or senior management team must consider the information from a range of sources and perspectives. If a balanced view does not appear to be available, it will be necessary to return to the data gathering process. It is not intended that this approach is used for on-going maintenance activities but for new areas for expansion, areas for regeneration or for closedown. The models represent different types in that some do little to suggest the way forward but simply piece together information whereas others suggest strategies which might be adopted by the school. The reader can use one or more of these models to build up a strategic picture of the school.

1 Boston Consulting Group matrix

The Boston Consulting Group (BCG) matrix was devised for the analysis of strategic positioning and strategic development in business units within large companies. We believe that the process can usefully be

Figure 5.2 BCG matrix.

employed to bring together information about strategic positioning and strategic possibilities within a school. The matrix is shown in Figure 5.2 and can be explained as follows:

- A product can be defined as a *star* if it has a high market share in a growing market. A good example from the business world is Microsoft. The company is the leading provider of software operating systems in a growing market. It has a very high market share in a rapidly expanding market. Its products would be located in the top left hand corner of the matrix. In the case of stars, the product may be supported by considerable investment. This is felt to be worthwhile in order to maintain the lead in the market.
- A product is considered to be a *problem* child (or question mark) if it is positioned in a growing market but there is doubt whether the product will be successful in terms of its competition with other products. Thus, if a large amount of resource is expended and the success of that investment is not yet known then the product may end up as a star (if successful) or a dog (if unsuccessful). At the present time a question mark hangs over that investment. Many new product launches are in this category initially.
- A *cash cow* has a high market share in a mature, low growth market. Little investment is needed in these more stable conditions and, because of the high market share, unit costs should remain below those of the competitors. The products that are cash cows therefore bring in more income than they expend so that they provide the 'cash' to maintain the products in the other segments of the matrix. The well-established products of the major tobacco companies can be considered to be cash cows as they bring in a steady income, until the consumer dies!
- *Dogs* are in the unfortunate position of having a low market share in a stable or declining market. They tend to drain human and financial resources, largely because of diseconomies of scale and, therefore, high unit costs. A good example would be vinyl records when CDs were introduced.

A school using this BCG approach would use the strategic data which it has obtained in order to locate its products on the matrix. Although, for convenience, we have placed items in discrete quadrants, in practice a product may be located on the borderline between two or more quadrants. In our case examples for secondary and primary schools, we have identified several school 'products' and located them on the matrix.

Case example 5.2: secondary school BCG

The school has experienced a sustained and significant increase in pupils in the sixth form studying psychology. This could be considered to be a star product as there seems to be a growing market for this subject for a wide variety of careers and, within the range of A levels offered, it is taking an increasing share of option preferences. There are significant indications that more pupils are staying on because this option is available in the school.

The school's problem child is its move to develop a greater focus on independent learning for pupils using various forms of information technology. At the moment it is a growing area with more and more quality software and other applications becoming available. The school is, however, having to invest heavily in this development when it is short of resources. Also, the reluctance of teachers and parents to see this as an alternative to traditional teaching has meant that it takes a very low share of total learning and teaching time. Either the move to develop this area will lead to a significant expansion of both the range and quality of learning opportunities or it will become an expensive bolt-on facility to the traditional learning curriculum.

The cash cows can be considered to be GCSE teaching in English and maths. The school is increasingly being judged on its literacy and numeracy outcomes at 16. Quality provision in these two subjects will ensure continued parental choice of the school and, hence, funding through the pupil unit component of the school budget.

Like many organisations, the school has a few products which might be classified as 'dogs'. Here it is the school meals service. The school is situated near the middle of the town centre and pupils can choose from many alternative food sources at lunchtime. The present meals service is seen as expensive and the choices offered do not meet pupil expectations.

Stars	Problem Children
A level Psychology	IT based independent learning
Cash Cows	**Dogs**
GCSE English and Maths teaching Years 10–11	School meals

Figure 5.3 BCG matrix: secondary example.

Case example 5.3: primary school BCG

The star, as far as the school is concerned, is its information technology provision. It has invested heavily in turning its library area into a learning resource centre with a significant number of multi-media machines linked to the Internet. It has also organised a deal with a computer supplier for parents to buy a lap-top computer for their children over a three-year period. It is seen by parents as the leading school in the growing area of technology and, as a result, is significantly oversubscribed.

The problem child for this school is its literacy programme. Decisions are needed about the most effective way to proceed as other schools already have a significant advantage in this area. The school has no option as to whether to develop this area so it must decide where to invest its resources to achieve high levels of literacy, especially for those whose reading age is below their chronological age. It is investigating several approaches: 'Successmaker' as a technology-based option; the staff-intensive Reading Recovery approach from New Zealand; THRASS (Teaching Handwriting, Reading and Spelling Skills). These options have considerable resource implications but should achieve significantly higher literacy scores in the government's target setting process. The key questions to resolve, however, concern which option or combination and at what resource level.

The school's cash cow is basic numeracy. The school has excellent learning schemes and achieves very good results in this area at Key Stage 1. As a result it retains a good impression with parents and secures an excellent intake for the school.

The dog product in this school is peripatetic music. The whole concept of extracting pupils for music tuition is disliked by children but the tutors are not available at any other time. Parents are increasingly dissatisfied with the quality of provision and the lack of stability of staffing so they are seeking alternative provision in the community. The school will need to decide whether this area is worthwhile now that the government requires the school to focus on literacy and numeracy.

Stars	Problem Children
Information technology	Reading recovery programmes
Cash Cows	**Dogs**
Basic numeracy teaching up to Key Stage I	Peripatetic music

Figure 5.4 BCG matrix: primary example.

The use of the BCG matrix

In both the primary and secondary examples, the strategic purpose of the activity is threefold. First, it provides a means of integrating the data gathered in the strategic analysis in order to determine the current position of key elements of the school's activities. Second, it focuses attention on action that needs to be undertaken to maintain star positioning, to ensure that problem children move to the left and not down to the dog category, to reinforce the core cash cow activities and, finally, to either damage limit or eliminate items in the dog category. Third, the matrix can be used as a means of articulating what the school believes its products will be in five years' time and which categories they will be in; most significantly it should identify the problem children that require investment and development in the near future.

Exercise 5.2: developing a BCG analysis

As a member of the Senior Management Team:

1   Identify the products, in your school, which have been raised for one reason or another in the strategic analysis, e.g. success, failure, unit cost high or low, popular or unpopular.
2   Place these products in the appropriate parts of the matrix in Figure 5.5.
3   Discuss the reasons and implications with the Senior Management Team.

Stars	**Problem Children**
Cash Cows	**Dogs**

Figure 5.5 Blank BCG matrix.

2 General Electric Screen

The General Electric (GE) Screen or Industry Attractiveness Matrix can be used by a school as a tool for gaining an aggregated strategic view of its position. It allows the school to analyse its provision against two categories of factors:

Factors relating to sector/market attractiveness:

market size
profit margins
competition
growth rate
supplier power

Factors relating to relative business strength:

relative market share
management skills
product/service quality
reputation
location

These two groups of factors can be used as axes on a matrix (in a similar way to Little's Lifecycle on page 91) although we have decided not to replicate such a matrix model but to use the concept of the two sets of criteria to aggregate the strategic analysis information, in this case for a primary school.

Case example 5.4: A GE Screen for a primary school

Brentwich Primary School has interpreted the business descriptors into the following educational framework:

Sector/Market Attractiveness	Interpreted Criteria
Market size	The number of pupils starting school over the next 5 years.
Profit margins	Results in (i) literacy and numeracy (ii) Key Stage 1 and 2 results
Competition	Other competing primary schools – state and independent
Growth rate	Increase in value-added
Supplier (or client) power	Parental and community attitude to the school

Figure 5.6 Market attractiveness criteria for Brentwich Primary School.

Relative Business Strength	Interpreted Criteria
Relative market share	Percentage of pupils in the catchment area attending the school
Management skills	Leadership and management skills of senior staff and subject leaders
Product/service quality	Quality of learning and teaching
Reputation	Reputation of the school in the community and media
Location	The attractiveness of the school's situation

Figure 5.7 Relative business strength criteria for Brentwich Primary School.

As part of the strategic analysis, the school collected data from four groups: the senior management team, classroom teachers, the parents and the governors and asked them to rate the school on a 1–10 scale on each of the criteria. The outcomes were:

MARKET ATTRACTIVENESS

	Senior Management Team	Teachers	Parents	Governors
Market size	8	8	6	6
Results (profit margins)	7	7	4	5
Competition	6	5	8	5
Growth rate	7	8	6	5
Supplier (or client) power	8	7	6	7

Figure 5.8 GE Screen analysis for Brentwich Primary School – market attractiveness.

RELATIVE BUSINESS STRENGTH

	Senior Management Team	Teachers	Parents	Governors
Relative market share	5	7	6	5
Management skills	7	7	4	4
Product/ service quality	4	7	6	4
Reputation	7	6	7	6
Location	4	3	8	5

Figure 5.9 GE Screen analysis for Brentwich Primary School — relative business strength.

The school should focus on where there are low scores or, very significantly, where there is a different perception by the different groups. Examples of the differences would be the perception of the results of the school between the senior management and teachers on one side and the parents and governors on the other. This would merit serious attention as would management skills. It can be seen that this tool not only provides a means of bringing together the data and highlighting areas for attention in terms of high and low scores but it shows the different perceptions of the various stakeholder groups.

Exercise 5.3 General Electric Screen analysis

As a member of the senior management team, use the blank matrices below to rate your school against the criteria using the scoring of 1–10. Then try to do the same using information from other participants' viewpoint.

MARKET ATTRACTIVENESS

	Senior Management Team	Teachers	Parents	Governors
Market size				
Results (profit margins)				
Competition				
Growth rate				
Supplier (or client) power				

Figure 5.10 Blank matrix for market attractiveness.

RELATIVE BUSINESS STRENGTH

	Senior Management Team	Teachers	Parents	Governors
Relative market share				
Management skills				
Product/ service quality				
Reputation				
Location				

Figure 5.11 Blank matrix for relative business strength.

3 Macro SWOT

Many schools or subject areas have used a SWOT analysis which considers strengths, weaknesses, opportunities and threats. Usually, the strengths and weaknesses are related to internal factors and the opportunities and threats relate to the external environment. The tool can be used as a method for drawing together information from a variety of techniques – a macro approach – as well as in the usual way to focus on a particular product or aspect of provision. A SWOT format can be used to compile a macro picture from all the evidence gained through strategic analysis. This does not simply involve filling in the details from the data, but requires that senior leaders in the school consider the validity of the data gathered so that it provides valuable information. It is thus a more rational approach than the subjective use of the tool simply to gather stakeholders' perceptions.

The SWOT approach is quick and easy and does not require any special skill or equipment in order to carry it out or to analyse it. The tool can be made more sophisticated by introducing sub-categories against which to place the information. This overcomes the criticism that, because of their diversity, the results cannot easily be summarised or aggregated. The information is not weighted so care must be taken in interpretation otherwise minor and major issues may be given equal prominence. Unlike Little's Lifecycle Analysis (see page 91), the process does not suggest any strategies other than the possibility of turning weaknesses into strengths and threats into opportunities.

In our case example, we have used some of the sub-categories which we suggest earlier in this chapter as aspects of the school's provision which should be covered by the data-gathering process.

Internal factors

- Curriculum
- Learning and teaching
- Assessment and results
- Extra-curricular activities
- Discipline and appearance
- Financial resources
- Premises
- Staffing, staff skills and abilities
- Governors
- Ethos/culture

External factors

- Political, legal and economic factors
- Central/local educational changes
- Demographic and socio-cultural trends
- Employment trends
- Technology
- Customers
- Other providers

Case example 5.5: a SWOT matrix for Shrewbridge School

At Shrewbridge School, the data gathering exercise has been summarised in the following chart.

	Strengths	**Weaknesses**
Curriculum	Literacy and language	Creative arts Numeracy
Learning and teaching	Variety of approaches and resources available	Differentiation Extension materials for the more able
Assessment and results	Good use of baseline entry data Steadily rising results in English	Targeting of individuals Maths results level over last 3 years
Extra-curricular activities	Sport	Few music or drama activities
Discipline and appearance	Clear behaviour policy	Inconsistent application of rewards and sanctions Unclear uniform policy
Financial resources	Balanced budget over last 2 years PTA income of £3000 per year	Lack of partnership with community to attract other funds
Premises	Welcoming entrance and reception area	Toilets need refurbishing
Staffing, staff skills and abilities	Stable staff with a little turnover	Inconsistent application of policies
Governors	Regularly attend meetings and school functions	Staff unhappy about their presence in lessons
Ethos/culture	Happy, willing pupils	Lack of shared vision and values, especially amongst staff

	Opportunities	Threats
Political, legal and economic factors	Targeted-funds and support for numeracy	Fewer quality teachers entering or remaining in the profession
Central/local educational changes	Further rationalisation of the core curriculum	Possibility of a new school on the other boundary of the estate Increased focus on achievement of numeracy targets
Demographic and socio-cultural trends	New estate and new industrial complex should increase the local population	Cost of houses may mitigate against the families who might use this school
Employment trends	New developments in the area	Workers may commute because of the cost of housing
Technology	To harness technology to raise standards of numeracy	Cost and lack of staff skills
Customers	Community networks available to improve communication	Pressure to provide a wider range of art, music and drama facilities
Other providers	Dissemination of literacy skills to other providers within the region	Community perceptions and hopes of a new school

Figure 5.12 Completed SWOT matrix.

Exercise 5.4 Building a macro SWOT for a school

Use this form to bring together the information which you have about your school from a strategic perspective.

	Strengths	**Weaknesses**
Curriculum		
Learning and teaching		
Assessment and results		
Extra-curricular activities		
Discipline and appearance		
Financial resources		
Premises		
Staffing, staff skills and abilities		
Governors		
Ethos/culture		

	Opportunities	Threats
Political, legal and economic factors		
Central/local educational changes		
Demographic and socio-cultural trends		
Employment trends		
Technology		
Customers		
Other providers		

Figure 5.13 Blank SWOT matrix.

4 Kawasaki's matrix

In his book *How to Drive the Competition Crazy*, Guy Kawasaki (1995) draws on a number of his experiences from the corporate world with Apple Computers. We have adapted one of his models to use as a strategic analysis tool. We use it to interpret data into what could be considered a feasible/desirable dimension which can be seen to operate as a matrix where the school's ability to provide (feasible) with the perceived value to the client (desirable) are set against one another as in Figure 5.14.

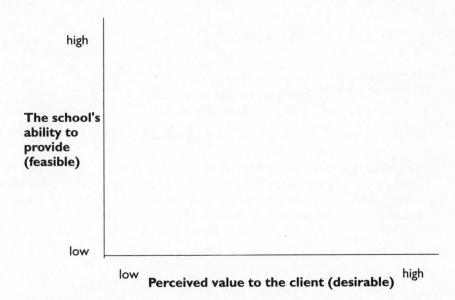

Figure 5.14 Kawasaki's matrix.
Source: Davies and Ellison, 1997, p. 216; adapted from Kawasaki, 1995, p. 76; itself based on Richey, 1994, pp. 47–51. Excerpted by permission of the original publisher, from *The Marketer's Visual Tool Kit* by Terry Richey. © 1994 Timberline Strategies Inc. Published by AMACOM, a division of American Management Association. All rights reserved.

Case example 5.6: a Kawasaki analysis of Lincoln School's provision

In Lincoln School the ability to provide sufficient high quality information technology facilities is moderate while parental expectations in this area are high. Similarly, while parents may consider Saturday morning games as very desirable, the ability of the school to persuade staff to work on Saturday mornings is limited. The school can offer after-school music provision to a high standard and parents are happy with this. This situation is summarised in Figure 5.15.

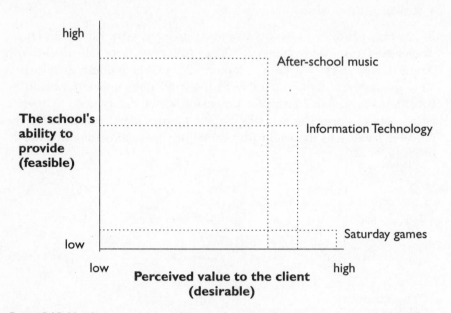

Figure 5.15 Matching provision and parental expectations.

This type of analysis can be seen to develop some of the choice characteristics explained in Chapter 6 in that it not only relates the strategic position between provider and receiver but defines the feasibility and suitability of such an option.

Exercise 5.5 A Kawasaki Analysis

From the information which you have about your school:

i   determine the features that you wish to analyse;
ii   decide on the school's ability to provide those features;
iii   decide on the desirability of those features in the eyes of the parents and pupils;
iv   position the features on the matrix;
v   study the position of the features. Those that are high and to the right are the key ones in which the school can demonstrate effectiveness and the customer is keen to accept the feature. Those which are high and to the left may need special consideration in the planning and marketing process if the customer is to change his/her attitude to their value. For those features which appear elsewhere, the school needs to decide on the appropriate strategic alternatives.

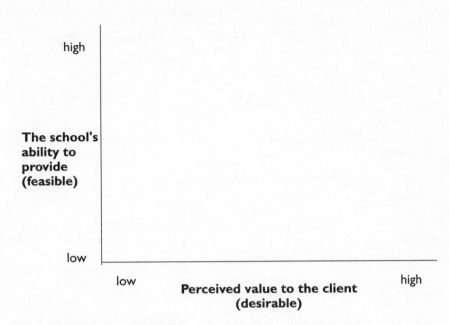

Figure 5.16 Blank Kawasaki matrix.

5 Little's Lifecycle Portfolio matrix

The Arthur D. Little organisation developed this matrix which is used in commerce and industry. When working with senior managers in schools who already have quite a high level of understanding of the planning process, we have found this tool to be of particular value. It provides a new way of assembling information and, rightly, promotes considerable discussion about the way forward.

A number of factors are considered and information is placed on one of the two axes of a matrix. When examining a particular aspect of provision, the vertical axis relates to the *competitive position* of the school in relation to other relevant educational provision. The descriptors for this position are: dominant, strong, favourable, tenable or weak. The horizontal axis relates to the *stages of maturity* of the aspect of provision being considered. The descriptors here range from embryonic through growth and mature to ageing. Thus, a blank matrix looks like this:

Stages of Maturity

	Embryonic	Growth	Mature	Ageing
Dominant				
Strong				
Favourable				
Tenable				
Weak				

Competitive Position (vertical axis label)

Figure 5.17 Little's Lifecycle Portfolio matrix.

The criteria by which the positions are determined for the *competitive position* axis are:

Dominant: The organisation often has a quasi- or legalised monopoly status.

Strong: The organisation can follow its own strategies without concern about the competition.

Favourable: The organisation is one of several leaders.

Tenable: The organisation's position can be maintained by specialisation or focus.

Weak: The organisation is too small to survive independently in the long term.

The criteria by which the positions are determined for the *stages of maturity* axis are:

Market growth rate

Growth potential
Breadth of product lines
Number of competitors

Spread of market share between competitors
Customer loyalty
Entry barriers
Technology

The stages of maturity are thus characterised as:

Embryonic:	through *growth* and *mature* to:	*Ageing*:

Embryonic:

- Rapid growth
- Changes in technology
- Fragmented market shares

- Pursuit of new customers

Ageing:

- Falling demand
- Declining number of customers and competitors
- Narrow product line

The Little organisation goes on to suggest strategies for products or services which are located in certain sectors of the matrix. We have adapted their suggestions in the grid below in Figure 5.18.

Stages of Maturity

		Embryonic	Growth	Mature	Ageing
	Dominant	Grow quickly	Grow quickly Attain cost leadership Defend position	Defend position Attain cost leadership Revitalise Grow quickly	Defend position Focus Revitalise
	Strong	Differentiate Grow quickly	Grow quickly Catch up Attain cost leadership Differentiate	Attain cost leadership Revitalise Differentiate/ focus Grow with other providers	Hold niche Find niche Hang-in
Competitive Position	**Favourable**	Differentiate Focus Grow quickly	Differentiate/ focus Catch-up Grow with other providers	Hold niche, hang-in Differentiate/ focus/find niche Revitalise Turnaround performance Grow with other providers	Retrench Turnaround performance
	Tenable	Grow with other providers Focus	Catch-up Hold niche, hang-in Focus or find niche Turnaround performance Grow with other providers	Turnaround performance Find niche Retrench	Divest parts of the work Retrench
	Weak	Find niche Catch-up Grow with other providers	Turnaround performance Retrench	Withdraw entirely Divest parts of the work	Withdraw entirely

Figure 5.18 Strategies suggested by Little's Lifecycle Portfolio matrix.

A school would use the matrix to consider an area of its work, such as after-school provision or A level Music. At the local level, the concept could also be used to analyse the position of each school in the district. Whatever the case, the position on the matrix suggests alternative strategies which might be appropriate. The examples below show how this might work in practice.

Case example 5.7: nursery provision for 0 to 4 year-olds on a primary or secondary school site

Greenfield School has a nursery unit which occupies a spare classroom. The nursery has an excellent reputation for developing literacy and numeracy skills. Over the last two years it has proved difficult to recruit good teachers to the main school but the presence of the nursery has been a deciding factor for several staff whose children are aged 0 to 3. Greenfield's position near a commuter station offers significant opportunities. The caretaker's house is available should extra space be needed.

1   *Decide on the aspect* under consideration, in this case the nursery.

2   Using the information gathered from a range of sources during strategic analysis, *decide on the competitive position* of the nursery.

The nursery is one of several in the area which have been quite successful in the last three years in terms of recruitment and reputation. This puts it in a *favourable* position.

3   *Decide the stage of maturity* of the nursery age market in your area.

There seems to be some potential *growth* in this age range because of government initiatives related to education and to women in the workforce.

4   *Place* the nursery *on the matrix.*

In this example, the nursery would be placed at point 1 on Figure 5.19 on page 96. It may also be appropriate to mark with an arrow the direction in which the aspect of provision seems to be moving on the matrix. The model now offers possible strategies according to the position in the matrix.

5   *Examine the suggested strategies.*

The matrix in Figure 5.18 on page 94 would suggest that this school should differentiate/focus, catch-up or grow with other providers.

Case example 5.8: GNVQ leisure and tourism

Redroof School has been running GNVQ courses in Business and Finance for three years and started Leisure and Tourism last year. The local FE college has been offering the latter course for two years and has a significant reputation for its provision.

1 *Decide on the aspect* under consideration, in this case the GNVQ Leisure and Tourism.

2 Using the information gathered from a range of sources during strategic analysis, *decide on the competitive position* of this course.

The school has little experience in this subject area. This puts it in a *tenable* position in terms of student recruitment and staff competence.

3 *Decide the stage of maturity* of the market for this course in your area.

This is a relatively new aspect of provision with the likelihood of considerable growth. This places the course in the *embryonic* category.

4 *Place* the course *on the matrix.*

In this example, the course would be placed at point 2 on Figure 5.19. It may also be appropriate to mark with an arrow the direction in which the aspect of provision seems to be moving on the matrix. The model now offers possible strategies according to the position in the matrix.

Stages of Maturity

		Embryonic	Growth	Mature	Ageing
Competitive Position	Dominant				
	Strong				
	Favourable		①		
	Tenable	②			
	Weak				

Figure 5.19 Positioning the examples of the Lifecycle Portfolio matrix.

5   *Examine the suggested strategies.*

The matrix in figure 5.18 on page 94 would suggest that this school should grow with the other providers or focus.

Information from other tools in this section should assist the school to further define the situation and help to focus the decision-making process.

The matrix can now be used to plot the position of the various aspects of your school's provision in order to stimulate debate and discussion about possible strategic options.

Conclusion

This chapter has shown, initially, how to collect data and, in the second part, how to put that data into a usable, analysable form through deploying five strategic analysis tools. It is possible to use some or all of these, although we feel that, in order to obtain a balanced view, schools should use at least three of the tools so that they can bring together information in different sorts of formats.

The first three strategic tools provide three key functions. They provide a means of integrating the data gathered in the data gathering exercises in order to show the current position of key elements of the school's activities. They focus attention on action that might be needed in order to achieve organisational success and they help to articulate what the school believes its strategic direction and products should be in the future.

The fourth tool, Kawasaki's matrix, helps to position various strategic options on a feasibility/desirability dimension which will lead into the choice process in Chapter 6. Finally, readers may find Little's Lifecycle Analysis useful in order to suggest strategies which the school could pursue in a range of situations.

Having established a clear strategic analysis perspective, and generated a series of options or alternatives, the organisation is now presented with a difficult task of choosing between them. This problem of choice is dealt with in the next chapter.

References

Abbott, R., Steadman S. and Birchenhough M. (1988) *GRIDS School Handbooks*, 2nd edn, Primary and Secondary versions, York: Longman for the SCDC.
Bowman, C. and Asch, D. (1987), *Strategic Management*, Basingstoke: Macmillan.
Davies B. (1997) 'Rethinking the educational context: a reengineering approach' in B. Davies and L. Ellison, *School Leadership for the 21st Century: A Competency and Knowledge Approach*, London: Routledge.

Davies, B. and Ellison, L. (1993) 'Parental Choice and School Response' paper presented at the British Educational Management and Administration Society, National Research Conference, Sheffield, February.

Davies, B. and Ellison, L (1997a) *School Leadership for the 21st Century: A Competency and Knowledge Approach*, London: Routledge.

Davies, B. and Ellison, L (1997b) *Strategic Marketing for Schools*, London: Pitman.

Glatter, R., Woods, P. and Bagley, C. (1995) *Diversity, Differentiation and Hierarchy: School Choice and Parental Preferences*, ESRC/CEPAM Invitation Seminar, Milton Keynes, 7–8 June.

Kawasaki, G. (1995) *How to Drive Your Competition Crazy*, New York: Hyperion.

Porter, M. (1980) *Competitive Strategy*, New York: Free Press.

West, A. (1992) 'Factors Affecting Choice of School for Middle Class Parents: Implications for Marketing', *Educational Management and Administration*, Vol. 20 No. 4: 223–230.

Chapter 6

Choice of strategy
Strategic plan or strategic intent?

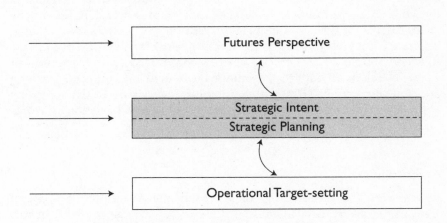

The purpose of the strategic analysis was to obtain an understanding of the school and the wider environment in which it functions. Once the information has been gathered and made accessible through building an aggregated strategic view, then a number of areas will be identified that require attention over the medium-term. From these areas, a number of possible strategic projects or activities will be generated. The senior team in a school then has to decide which activities are appropriate to pursue and then to divide them into those which have definable detailed strategies and outcomes in the immediate future and those which require the school to build capability and understanding around a strategic intent as a framework for action in the future.

Factors in the choice process

How can the school initially assess whether the activity is one that should be pursued and, second, whether it is one that is capable of immediate structured planning or one where capability must be built around a strategic intent? Three key factors can be used to aid this process. They are the questions of: *suitability, acceptability* and *feasibility*. We will examine each in turn.

Suitability

A key criterion for judging that a course of action is suitable would be whether it exploits the opportunities identified in the strategic analysis. This will allow the school to capitalise on the positive aspects of its situation. The proposed course of action should also deal with any threats posed to the school so that they are minimised or, better still, turned into opportunities. It should seek to utilise and build on the strengths of the school and help to reduce any weaknesses so that, ultimately, they become areas of strength. Most importantly, the course of action should fit in with the school's core purposes. This would, for example, relate all activities to the achievement of enhanced learning outcomes by pupils. In a sense, suitability acts as an initial screening approach to consider whether the proposed course of action is worth pursuing further.

Acceptability

In assessing the acceptability of a chosen alternative, the concept of 'organisational fit' can be utilised. One factor that is involved in this assessment could be the way in which the new project or development fits in with existing systems. Is there little change or disturbance or is there likely to be a degree of turbulence and organisational stress as new ways of operating take time to settle down? This analysis can be extended to examine how the proposed course of action affects the functions of the different curricular areas, groups or individuals within the school. An important factor to consider is how far the proposed course of action meets the expectations of the various stakeholder groups that form the school community in its widest sense. Will the action move the school in the direction expected and thus gain support or will it move it in a way that will cause friction with these groups? The financial effect will also be a significant factor to consider. Can the action contribute to increased pupil numbers or draw in other sources of finance leading to a surplus, or will it lead to the school exceeding its original budget targets? Last, but not least, is the concept of risk. Is there a high probability of success with the course of action? Or is there a degree of risk that the desired outcome will not be met? If the latter is the case, then the acceptability of that degree of risk to the various stakeholder groups needs to be very carefully considered.

Feasibility

In deciding whether the proposed strategic option is a feasible one for the school, a number of questions need to be considered. First, if the option has a resource expenditure element then the obvious question needs asking, can the strategy be funded? Are other resources available? If there is to be a significant increase in the performance of the school's personnel, then questions focusing on their ability to perform at the required level need to be asked. If there is a likely problem with the levels of performance required, then the school needs to focus on how the necessary skills can be secured. Similarly, if extra demands are to be placed on the physical assets of the school, such as space or equipment, consideration needs to be given to whether this is feasible. In particular, attention needs to focus on the appropriate technology which would be needed to support the proposed developments. If the school is in a competitive position with other schools then it needs to consider whether the necessary market position can be achieved. The competitive reaction of other organisations, especially local schools, to a particular proposal is a very significant factor. Many options are considered to be not feasible because the school feels that it cannot cope with the adverse reactions to its plans.

Using the key questions of suitability, acceptability and feasibility the school will be able to identify some courses of action which it should pursue and those which should be disregarded. The next stage is to determine whether the courses of action chosen are ones for which a strategic plan can be written or ones where a process of strategic intent needs to be articulated. First, is it feasible to proceed with a clearly defined plan over a set number of years? If so, then more detailed strategic planning can begin. Thus, for those projects that are predictable, such as aspects of refurbishment, the school will go through a choice process to prioritise them into the strategic plan. A similar process will be required in order to ensure that the component parts of major projects, such as a new building, are sequenced logically as part of the school's development. If this type of rational and predictable planning is not an appropriate approach, then the second level of feasibility can be considered. The school asks whether, in order for the strategy to become a feasible as well as a suitable and desirable option, the school needs to articulate a strategic intent and build capability until the required course of action becomes clearer and more attainable. A strategic intent must be formed within the school for those areas for which it needs to build the capability to understand, and the ability to deal with, in the future. Examples of such intents were shown in Chapter 4 on page 55.

Assessing possible courses of action for strategic planning: a decision-making matrix

In the case of strategic planning, it is likely that a series of possible projects or courses of action will have been identified, rather than just one. How then can a choice be made between them, especially when they are not necessarily alternative means to the same end? One approach is to adapt a decision-making tool used by Johnson and Scholes (1993: 304) which analyses an organisation's existing capability against that required to implement a proposed course of action and to use this to inform decision-making. The model gives information to aid decision-making, rather than pointing to the 'best' solution. In our adaptation we use the term 'capability' rather than 'capacity' and focus on the difference between present capability and that required for the proposed new activity. The school can then assess the significance of the current and projected position before choosing a course of action.

Case example 6.1: Lincoln School

In Figure 6.1 it can be seen that Lincoln School is considering three strategic planning developments: extending and expanding technology provision (Strategy A); extending the range of after school activities (Strategy B); and building a minor extension to the school to create an extra classroom (Strategy C). The case example school now proceeds through six stages:

Stage one

This involves creating a list of the key capability factors which should be considered in the decision-making analysis. In column (a) of Figure 6.1 we have used an adapted version of the factors given by Johnson and Scholes (1993: 304). This is only one possible list of factors and readers may wish to use alternative headings or groupings that they think are more appropriate.

Stage two

Lincoln School has already undertaken a strategic analysis. It has interpreted the information from that analysis and used it to form a rating of its current position in relation to the key capability factors. This rating is created on a 0 to 5 scale. The results of this analysis are recorded in column (b) of Figure 6.1. The following thinking informed the Lincoln School example:

(a) Key capability factors		(b) Current school situation	Key capability factors – Implication (c)		
			Strategy A (extend technology provision)	Strategy B (extend range of after school activities)	Strategy C (building extension)
Financial	Available cash	1			
	Ability to raise additional funds	2			
Physical	Well maintained premises	3			
	Up-to-date equipment	2			
Human	Skilled staff	3			
	Quality of leadership & management	4			
Other	Reputation for quality education	3			
	Community/business/educational contacts	2			
Optional	School culture	4			
	Pupil attitude/commitment	3			

(NB) 0 = limited resource or capability and/or unimportant, 5 = extensive resource or capability and/or critical to success of strategy.

Figure 6.1 Capability analysis.

Financial The school has only minimal cash reserves and on a 0 to 5 scale would only rate itself 1. Its immediate ability to raise additional funds is reasonable if it could energise its relationships with parents and the local business community which have lain dormant for the last two years. Assessing the current position, a 2 rating would be allocated but it is felt that this could be improved.

Physical The buildings are well-maintained but rather dated so the school would rate itself 3 on this criterion. However, the general equipment in the school is in need of up-dating and replacing so it would only rate itself 2 in this category.

Human The staff of the school has experienced a degree of turnover bringing in new skills, and an extensive staff development programme has been initiated. As a result the school considers a 3 rating is appropriate here. The recently reformed senior leadership comprises a headteacher who supplemented her NPQH management training with an International MBA in Educational Leadership. The deputy head also has a specialist degree at Masters level in Leadership and Management and has extensive experience of this. The senior team also includes the school finance manager. A programme of middle management development has been initiated in the school. As a result, leadership and management is rated at 4.

Other The school has a solid, if uninspiring, reputation for the quality of the education which it provides and rates itself 3 in this category. Its links with the wider community need significantly improving and it could only rate itself 2 in this category.

Optional School culture is notoriously difficult to define but we shall use the idea of a good attitude to change and development within a positive set of working relationships that focus on the organisation's aims. In this context the senior staff believe that this has undergone significant improvement and would rate it as a 4. The attitude of pupils and their commitment to the school is good but not extensive, so a rating of 3 would be allocated here.

Stage three

At this stage the school determines the *required* situation in relation to each of the key capability factors for each of the proposed strategies (A, B, C).

Below we examine the three possible strategies that Lincoln School is considering and the capability requirements that they throw up. The figures can then be placed in the three parts of column (c) in Figure 6.1.

UNDERTAKING STRATEGY A: EXTENDING TECHNOLOGY PROVISION IN
THE SCHOOL

In its desire to improve technology provision, the school seeks to continue the shift of the library from a book-centred activity to a community
learning resource centre by the purchase of additional multi-media
computers and to integrate the use of this technology into all aspects
of the curriculum. It would rate the necessary capability factors as
follows:

Financial The school needs *more* cash for this purchase. In these
circumstances it would put a rating of 3 on the need for available
cash. The limited ability to raise extra funds needs to be remedied
and therefore it would have to increase its capability for fund-raising
to 4.

Physical The project would require adequate levels of premises maintenance so a rating of 3 would be given but the necessary shift to more
up-to-date equipment and an associated cabling system would mean a
5 in this category.

Human The staff would need further training and development on
how to integrate multi-media technology into the curriculum, so a
rating of 4 would be needed. The current level of leadership and
management ability in the school would be required in order to introduce these changes so a 4 rating would be used, the same as currently
exists.

Other The school reputation for the quality of the education would
have to be maintained at 3 for external support to be generated. Its
links with the wider community need significantly improving to
achieve sponsorship for this development so a 4 rating in this category
is necessary.

Optional School culture, in terms of its readiness to accept change,
needs to be maintained at 4. The attitude of pupils and their commitment to the school probably needs to be increased if independent
learning is to be developed, so a rating of 4 would be allocated here.

UNDERTAKING STRATEGY B: EXTENDING THE RANGE OF AFTER-SCHOOL
ACTIVITIES

The school wishes to offer a wider range of opportunities for its pupils
outside the formal teaching day by expanding the number of after-school

and other activities it offers. In increasing this provision it assesses the following resource and other changes that will be necessary:

Financial   The school only needs a limited amount of its general budget to provide for these activities so it decides to put a rating of 2 on this. It would need to raise additional extra funds from other sources and decides an increase in its capability to 3 in this category is needed.

Physical   The school would need higher levels of premises maintenance so there would be an increased rating of 4 in this category. The more up-to-date equipment required to facilitate some activities would mean a 3 in this category.

Human   The staff would not require any further skills beyond those that they have so a rating of 3 would be maintained. The existing level of leadership and management of the school is well able to motivate individuals and manage these changes so a 4 rating would be required, the same as previously.

Other   The reputation for the quality of the school's education would have to be maintained at 3 for external support to be generated. Its links with the wider community would have to be enhanced for some activities so a 3 rating in this category is necessary.

Optional   School Culture, in terms of the readiness to accept change, needs to be maintained at 4. The attitude of pupils and their commitment to the school probably needs to be increased if additional activities are to be undertaken, so a rating of 4 would be allocated here.

UNDERTAKING STRATEGY C: MINOR BUILDING EXTENSION

The school considers building a minor extension to create an extra classroom space.

Financial   The school needs to generate a significant extra amount of cash and in these circumstances it would put a rating of 4 on this. The lack of immediate financial resources highlights the urgent need to obtain extra funds externally to move ahead with this strategy, requiring an increase in capability to 5 in this category.

Physical   The comparison here is not applicable.

Human   The comparison here is not applicable.

Other   The school reputation for the quality of the education would have to be increased to generate extra external support so a rating of 4 would be made. Its links with the wider community need significantly improving to support this development so a 4 rating in this category is necessary.

Optional   The comparison here is not applicable.

Stage four

The ratings which result from the analysis in Stage three have been entered on Figure 6.2.

The difference between the school's capability, as shown in column (b) of Figure 6.2 and the project requirements, as shown in the three parts of column (c), is now calculated for each capability factor and each strategy. The figure has been placed in brackets on the matrix. For example, if the school rates the *required* capability in relation to 'available' cash necessary for strategy A as 3, then the difference between this and the *actual* school position (of 2) shows a mismatch.

Stage five

The differences between actual and required capability for each project then provides a framework for management analysis and decision-making. Instead of relying on assumptions and individual preferences, the management team has a set of criteria to analyse the necessary resource and other capability measures for each project. The critical factor to bear in mind is not that the strategy with the lowest possible mismatch is the automatic choice but that, in making choices, information of this nature is a critical factor. As was shown earlier, however, with Boisot's diagram (see page 57), intuition and insight will have to be used to inform this decision.

Stage six

Consider which projects should be taken forward.

Readers may now wish to apply the decision framework for proposed changes or development in their own schools. This can be achieved by undertaking Exercise 6.1 on page 110.

(a) Key capability factors	(b) Current school situation	Key capability factors – Implication (c)		
		Strategy A (extend technology provision)	Strategy B (extend range of after school activities)	Strategy C (building extension)
Financial				
Available cash	1	3 (2)	2 (1)	4 (3)
Ability to raise additional funds	2	4 (2)	3 (1)	5 (3)
Physical				
Well maintained premises	3	3 (0)	4 (1)	N/A
Up-to-date equipment	2	5 (3)	3 (1)	N/A
Human				
Skilled staff	3	4 (1)	3 (0)	N/A
Quality of leadership & management	4	4 (0)	4 (0)	N/A
Other				
Reputation for quality education	3	3 (0)	3 (0)	4 (1)
Community/business/educational contacts	2	4 (2)	3 (1)	4 (2)
Optional				
School culture	4	4 (0)	4 (0)	N/A
Pupil attitude/commitment	3	4 (1)	4 (1)	N/A

(NB) 0 = limited resource or capability and/or unimportant, 5 = extensive resource or capability and/or critical to success of strategy.

Figure 6.2 Capability analysis decision-making tool – school example.

(a)

(b)

(c)

| | | Key capability factors – Implication | | |
Key capability factors	Current school situation	Strategy A	Strategy B	Strategy C
Financial				
Available cash				
Ability to raise additional funds				
Physical				
Well maintained premises				
Up-to-date equipment				
Human				
Skilled staff				
Quality of leadership & management				
Other				
Reputation for quality education				
Community/business/educational				
Optional				
School culture				
Pupil attitude/commitment				

(NB) 0 = limited resource or capability and/or unimportant, 5 = extensive resource or capability and/or critical to success of strategy.

Figure 6.3 Proforma for decision-making.

Exercise 6.1: a capability analysis

1   Using Figure 6.3 on page 109 decide the various strategies which
     you wish to consider and enter them in A or B or C of column (c).
2   Decide if the factors in column (a) are appropriate for your school.
3   Complete the column headed (b) for your own school and also the
     A, B, C parts of column (c) for the proposed strategies.
4   Examine the results.
5   Consider the management implications and the capability require-
     ments for each project.

Drawing up the strategic plan and the strategic intent framework

Now that projects have been assessed against a range of criteria, decisions
will have to be made on which should be taken forward. Judgements are
needed about whether a particular project falls into the strategic planning
process or requires the process of building strategic intent. Let us now
look at a format for a strategic plan and a strategic intent framework.

Creating a strategic plan

The significant feature of a strategic plan is that it has definable goals
that have precise measurable outcomes that are SMART (specific, measurable, achievable, relevant and timed) and challenging. For the senior
leaders in the school it is a benchmark against which to measure individual yearly progress and a framework for re-articulating and refocus-
ing those individual year targets as progress either exceeds or falls short
of that which was planned.

   The danger inherent in strategic planning is that many of the doubtful
features of development planning may be repeated. It is important that
endless lists which are then sub-divided are avoided. Strategy, as we
have described it, is a process whereby major developments are articulated and the leader in the school can monitor the few rather than the
detail of the many. We see strategic planning in schools as having three
major interlinked components. These are:

1   The learning outcomes: pupil progress and achievement.
2   Support for the quality of learning and teaching processes.
3   Management arrangements: physical and financial resources, school
     structures and organisation.

To focus on the centrality of pupil progress, the relationship between
these elements should be seen as core purpose achieved through supportive activities and key enabling management activities. These can be
visualised as follows:

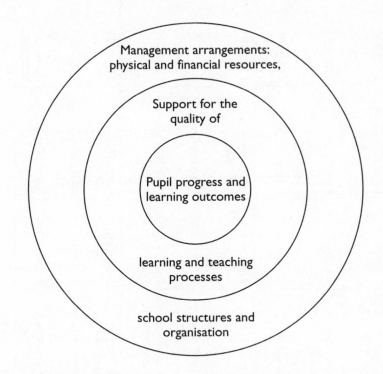

Figure 6.4 The centrality of pupil progress and learning outcomes.

These three areas allow the strategic leader to monitor a limited number of strategic plans – we suggest no more than three in each category, giving nine major strategic planning activities. In order to ensure that the projects are progressed, the following information will be needed for each:

- Time frame – when will that part of the strategic plan be achieved?
- Who has overall responsibility for the project?
- What are the costs involved and how will they be spread over the time period?

We have drawn up a strategic planning sheet for this which can be seen in Figure 6.5 (for a secondary school) and Figure 6.6 (for a primary school). The sheet will provide information which can be used for taking the school forward in the medium-term. The member of staff with responsibility for a project will then work with others to plan the detail of its implementation year by year and incorporate these stages into the relevant operational target-setting plans.

	Strategic planning area	Time frame	Responsibility?	Cost
The learning outcomes: pupil progress & achievement	1. Improve levels of literacy in Key Stage 3 – 80% pupils to reach level 5 by end of year 9: 50% to reach level 6.	3 years	Peter O'Sullivan	£120,000
	2. Raise standards of numeracy in Key Stage 4, all pupils to achieve a grade at GCSE; 65% to reach C or above.	4 years	Ken Davies	£100,000
	3. All pupils involved in at least two extra-curricular activities	3 years	Sandra Thody	£15,000
Support for the quality of learning & teaching processes	1. Improve quality of teaching in relation to OFSTED criteria	4 years	John West-Burnham	£20,000
	2. Develop more independent technology-based learning – implement Successmaker and the development of the Learning Grid	3 years	Caroline Brown	£30,000
	3. Ensure that all staff are skilled in target-setting and are supported by an efficient and accessible information system.	4 years	Mike Billingham	£70,000
Management arrangements: physical & financial resources, school structure & organisation	1. Technology equipment – increase level of provision: install 100 multi-media machines	3–5 years	Carol Short	£100,000
	2. Rewiring and refurbishment of lower school building (including ISDN links)	2–5 years	John Cain	£30,000
	3. Building extension – commission estimates, raise funds and start new 6th Form Centre	4 years	Ray McCann	Await estimates

Figure 6.5 A strategic plan for a secondary school.

	Strategic planning area	Time frame	Responsibility?	Cost over the time frame
The learning outcomes: pupil progress & achievement	1. Improve basic literacy – no more than 5% pupils with reading age below chronological age, at least 30% Year 6 achieving Level 5 English and 10% achieving Level 6.	3 years	Julia Barnett	£10,000
	2. Raise standards of numeracy – no more than 5% pupils achieving at less than SATs level for age, 30% Year 6 achieving Level 5 in maths	4 years	Peter Jones	£6000
	3. All pupils involved in at least two extra-curricular activities	3 years	Deborah Sinclair	£1000 + PTA funds
Support for the quality of learning & teaching processes	1. Improve general quality of teaching in line with OFSTED criteria	2–4 years	John Robertson	£2000
	2. Increase the level of computer software for pupil learning.	3 years	Viv Armstrong	£2000
	3. Improve staff access and ability to use IT for pupil tracking in the learning process	4 years	Deborah Sinclair	£10,000
Management arrangements: physical & financial resources, school structure & organisation	1. Technology equipment, increase level of provision	3–5 years	Viv Armstrong	£20,000 from external funds
	2. Rewiring and refurbishment of Key Stage 2 areas	4 years	John Robertson	£8000
	3. Building specialist nursery area – commission estimates, raise funds and start	4 years	John Robertson	External Grant

Figure 6.6 A strategic plan for a primary school.

Creating a strategic intent framework

This is different from creating a strategic plan which deals with the concrete and definable. This framework for strategic intent concentrates on the major aim of 'leveraging up' performance to a significantly higher level by building capability in the organisation. This capability enhancement is based on increased knowledge and understanding as to *how* to perform at a higher level as well as *what* to perform. So, for example, a strategic intent could be 'to create a high success and expectation culture in the school'. There must be a process of cultural understanding as to what is really necessary to change the organisation as well as shorter-term actions to improve performance. A good example is having a fundamental review of what it means to create a success culture in a school as against working to increase pass grades marginally.

In Chapter 4 we looked at strategic intent and readers may wish to refer back to that process now. We developed a strategic intent template with three elements:

i   A description of the strategic intent.
ii   An outline of the measures that are necessary to build capability to achieve that intent over a period of time.
iii Integrating the experience gained through the process of formulating understanding in ii so that, as a 'learning organisation', the intent can be reformulated and focused so that definitive outcomes can be achieved at a specific point.

The case example which follows provides a completed proforma for creating a strategic intent. This is shown in Figure 6.7

Intent	Capability-building measures	Move to strategic plan OR Reformulate intent
1. Create a high expectation and success culture	i. celebrate success ii. communicate targets iii. no failure culture iv. find something for each child to succeed at v. staff training to ensure the school reinforces the positive vi. focus success on teams vii. establish time period for activities and review date	At the end of a specified time period EITHER *capability will be established so that a clear understanding in detailed terms will be established and the school can move on to the strategic planning process in this area – this means that the WHAT of capability building measures turns into the HOW of strategic planning* OR *the capability building measures reframe the question of WHAT should be investigated so that a more focused capability building approach follows on*
2. Design and implement accurate performance indicators and hold everyone accountable for them	i. staff development on target-setting ii. create individual pupil, staff and organisational targets for day-to-day use iii. create information system to provide accurate assessments on demand iv. create self-reviewing teams v. build into appraisal system vi. investigate resources to support vii. establish time period for activities and review date	At the end of a specified time period EITHER *capability will be established so that a clear understanding in detailed terms will be established and the school can move on to the strategic planning process in this area – this means that the WHAT of capability building measures turns into the HOW of strategic planning* OR *the capability building measures reframe the question of WHAT should be investigated so that a more focused capability building approach follows on*
3. Establish technology-based individual learning for all pupils	i. scan environment for latest developments in technology ii. investigate devoting more curriculum time to study skills and independent learning skills for pupils	At the end of a specified time period EITHER *capability will be established so that a clear understanding in detailed terms will be established and the school can move on to the strategic planning*

	iii. create a culture where all staff are IT literate and integrate it into their teaching iv. investigate potential sponsorship and resource support v. establish time period for activities and review date	*process in this area – this means that the WHAT of capability building measures turns into the HOW of strategic planning* OR *the capability building measures reframe the question of WHAT should be investigated so that a more focused capability building approach follows on*
4. Build 'leadership in depth' throughout the staff	i. support staff to take on responsibility to deal with issues as they arise ii. provide leadership and management development for all staff iii. develop a 'no blame culture' where staff are encouraged to take risks iv. provide a forum for staff to discuss their roles in an ever-changing environment v. establish time period for activities and review date	At the end of a specified time period EITHER *capability will be established so that a clear understanding in detailed terms will be established and the school can move on to the strategic planning process in this area – this means that the WHAT of capability building measures turns into the HOW of strategic planning* OR *the capability building measures reframe the question of WHAT should be investigated so that a more focused capability building approach follows on*
5. Link home and school through the development of a learning community	i. set up discussion forum with community to consider the nature of the potential links ii. evaluate how open access, Internet, the Learning Grid and other technology creates a learning centre for the whole community all day and all year iii. investigate resources, possible funds, bidding strategies iv. create an Open Door culture v. establish time period for activities and review date	At the end of a specified time period EITHER *capability will be established so that a clear understanding in detailed terms will be established and the school can move on to the strategic planning process in this area – this means that the WHAT of capability building measures turns into the HOW of strategic planning* OR *the capability building measures reframe the question of WHAT should be investigated so that a more focused capability building approach follows on*

Figure 6.7 A strategic intent framework for a primary or secondary school.

Case example 6.1: Brentwich School

After undertaking a 'futures awareness' training session and an extensive strategic analysis, Brentwich School decided to focus on building strategic intent in a number of areas as shown in the first column of Figure 6.7. They then articulated a series of capability building measures to work on in the next 3–5 years. This will then either produce capability for action which can be translated into a definable plan *or* it will have redefined the challenge and more capability building will have to take place before the achievement of the intent is possible.

Conclusion

By using this chapter, the school should have the frameworks to enable it to be in a position to articulate a strategic plan which it can work on in a definable way while, at the same time, pursuing a number of strategic intents which will redefine its experience and planning process as organisational and individual capability is developed. It is now possible to move on to the final stage of our model, that of operational target-setting.

References

Johnson, G. and Scholes, K. (1993) *Exploring Corporate Strategy* 3rd edn, Hemel Hempstead: Prentice Hall.

Chapter 7

Operational target-setting
Establishing a framework

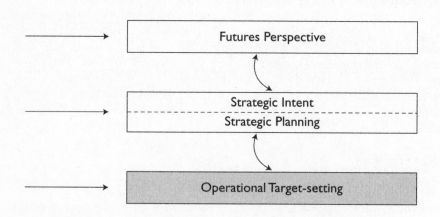

The focus on pupil progress and the raising of their achievement has become the key organisational objective for schools but it must be supported through appropriate learning and teaching strategies and management arrangements. These three aspects of the school's activities should be set out in an effective operational planning format. We see the traditional school development plan being replaced in two ways. The medium-term element will be subsumed into the strategic plan (as outlined in Chapter 6). The shorter-term elements will focus more directly on the raising of pupil achievement and, thus, will 'sharpen up' significantly the planning framework through much more focused operational target-setting plans at a range of levels within the school.

This chapter looks at this concept of operational target-setting plans which will ensure a demonstrable overall improvement in learning and outcomes for pupils over a 12- to 24-month timescale. The chapter considers the functions of operational target-setting plans, the key pointers to success in creating and implementing them and our proposed framework. Schools will need to decide on appropriate terminology for this shorter-term planning; we have used target-setting as this reflects the current emphasis in the UK.

The functions of operational target-setting plans

While schools must ensure continuous improvement in standards of achievement by pupils, simply stating the desired outcomes or targets will not ensure that they are achieved. An operational plan must also set out the processes which will support the achievement of the targets. It is important to distinguish between pupil progress and achievement towards particular outcomes (i.e. standards), the factors which bring this about (i.e. learning and teaching) and the management arrangements to support both of these. The school must begin by setting targets or goals for pupils' achievement and then develop appropriate learning and teaching strategies to reach these goals. An effective leadership and management framework must then be provided in support. The plans are then used to ensure that the proposed activities are scheduled, resourced and do, in fact, take place in an effective manner. Effective operational target-setting plans have a number of purposes which are outlined below.

1 Specifying targets

The planning process enables the school to set challenging yet attainable and measurable targets to support a continuous improvement in pupil learning outcomes. As the *Improving Schools* booklet (OFSTED 1994) points out, 'all schools, even the best, are capable of continuous improvement' and the White Paper, *Excellence in Schools* (DFEE 1997), reinforces this. The process of target-setting should encourage those in the school to look outwards to see what is being achieved elsewhere – in the world, not just in the UK. The factors relating to targets are discussed in more detail on pp. 121–5 and are developed in Chapters 8 and 9 by a primary head and by secondary strategic managers.

As well as specifying targets for pupil outcomes, the plan will also set out targets for developments in learning and teaching and for the management developments which are planned to support the achievement of the pupil outcomes.

2 Involving stakeholders

Many schools are now realising that the *process* of creating plans is vitally important for the achievement of the final *product* because it is through involvement in the development of plans that commitment is obtained for their realisation. Targets which have been agreed in advance are more likely to be achieved so it is particularly important to involve pupils and staff in negotiating those that relate to them. The planning process can also involve parents and the wider community in a partnership to raise achievement.

3 Prioritising tasks and focusing

Even after going through a process of strategic choice (as described in Chapter 6), there are still too many activities which could be planned. At this operational stage, decisions are made about which activities, especially in relation to learning and teaching and the learning context, are the most important in order to reach higher outcomes for pupils. The costing of various alternative courses of action will allow the school to inform its decision-making process through 'value for money' information. Thus, the prioritising and focusing of effort is a key function of the operational target-setting process.

4 Allocating resources

The achievement of the targets requires the allocation of appropriate and adequate resources. The published plans will set out the allocation of resources and provide clear guidelines for spending and a framework for monitoring that expenditure. It is important that the process of resource allocation should be seen as facilitating the educational process.

5 Facilitating change

An operational target-setting plan is a means of facilitating and driving through change in the school. It acts as a guide for those charged with the responsibility for carrying out the developments which are designed to allow the targets to be achieved. With a clear framework, staff can be supported to manage the changes by planning and prioritising their own work. The school can ensure that the staff are also supported in developing the appropriate skills and knowledge

6 Communicating

Operational target-setting plans communicate what needs to be done across a variety of areas by providing a means of articulating and co-ordinating priorities and targets to all stakeholders. There is, thus, a coherent picture of the school's activities. This is very important if staff are to set their work in curricular areas, year teams, houses, key stages and so on in the overall context of the whole school targets and priorities.

7 Monitoring

The plan can provide an effective instrument for monitoring progress both by those responsible for implementation and by those who have managerial oversight of the initiatives. A well thought out plan in which the targets are clearly specified, measurable and timed allows the school to assess where it is at various points in the year with respect to those targets. If targets do not appear to be going to be achieved, remedial action can be undertaken before it is too late.

8 Annual reviewing and evaluating

As a policy document approved by the governors, the whole school operational plan provides the basis of agreement and action by the stakeholders in the management of the school. By stating activities and targets, the plan provides a basis for annual review and it can, if required, provide the appraisal framework for senior leaders and other staff in the school. As part of the planning process the school must establish the structures and procedures by which this review will take place. As targets are achieved, new ones can be formulated for the next cycle of activity. Formal and planned evaluation can assist in the process of ensuring that the most effective means are chosen to reach the desired goals in the future.

9 External accountability

An operational target-setting plan provides part of the information for any external audit and evaluation of the school by the LEA or other external agency, such as OFSTED.

10 Recognition

A report on achievements or on progress towards targets can provide a major part of the information between the school and its stakeholders in signalling and proclaiming 'success'. The information can be disseminated at the governors' annual meeting, via newsletters or at parent/community activities.

Key pointers to success in operational target-setting plans

We are proposing a new perspective, not of a reconstituted school development plan, but of a differently focused plan for setting and achieving targets. It will thus provide the mechanism for meeting short-term (annual) pupil-focused achievement targets. Our interpretation of the operational plan is similar to that of Caldwell and Spinks (1992: 43) who point to the folly of creating 'a relatively immutable document' in an environment of rapid change. They refer instead to 'a relatively concise statement of priorities and strategies ... which is constantly reviewed' to take account of changes in the school's environment.

We feel that our approach can accommodate the criticism of planning made by Fullan who stated that 'the pursuit of planned change is a mug's game' because we exist in conditions of dynamic complexity so that 'most change is unplanned' (1993: 138). What we hope to demonstrate is that by having the school's values and strategic intent as 'signposts', the operational plan can be used to provide part of the path in the right direction and can ensure that progress is made. Also, in terms of turbulence or change in the environment, then a 12- to 24-month timescale does give reasonable stability. While the longer-term framework of strategic planning is possible in some areas of the school's activities, the concept of strategic intent is more powerful in other areas. Thus, we have considerable reservations about the validity of requests for five-year detailed costed development plans that have emerged from the inspection process. We believe that our model prevents an over-rigid approach by ensuring that, even while the operational plan is being created and implemented, there are people constantly scanning the environment in order to ensure that no valuable opportunities or shifts in direction are missed. We would also suggest that, despite the view of most staff, schools are relatively stable in terms of their *modus operandi*, staffing and budgets compared with most companies.

The features of operational target-setting plans

An operational target-setting plan should involve everyone at all levels in the school so it should comprise a range of targets such as:

- whole school targets which take account of national and local priorities;
- curricular area and other sub-unit targets;
- staff targets – in order to achieve the whole school targets;
- pupil targets – in order to ensure that performance is raised to an appropriate level.

A number of acronyms have been developed over the years in relation to targets. The DFEE (1997b) refers to SMART targets in which the A represents 'achievable' and the R represents 'realistic'. We feel that these two really refer to the same thing so, with the aid of our colleague John West-Burnham, we have built on an earlier version (Ellison and Davies

1990: 36) and developed a checklist which should help to gain commitment and to encourage achievement. What is important in a school is that a similar list is agreed and used as a checklist during the target-setting process. We feel that all targets should be:

- **S** pecific
- **M** easurable and monitored
- **A** chievable and agreed
- **R** elevant and resourced
- **T** imed
- **I** nteresting
- **E** xciting
- **S** uccess-orientated (and challenging)

Plans should be based on evidence gathered during the strategic analysis (in Chapter 5). They should focus on a limited number of targets in order to make it more likely that they are achieved. A 12- to 24-month period is appropriate with annual reviews.

Plans should be clear and unambiguous so that performance targets are clear and disagreement can be avoided. The layout of the document should show:

- details of the activities that contribute to achieving the strategic intent and the strategic plan;
- the cost of each activity;
- clear responsibilities for implementation and monitoring;
- clear success criteria for each target.

Plans should be live documents and should not lie unused on a shelf. They should be checked at frequent intervals and any necessary adjustments made.

We now move on to look in more detail at various aspects of targets and their setting. Whilst some general considerations relating to targets and target-setting are outlined here, more detail can be found in Chapters 8 and 9 and in government publications such as *Setting Targets to Raise Standards* (DFEE 1996) and *From Targets to Action* (DFEE 1997b).

Types of targets

Taberrer (1997) describes three types of targets which could be developed and which would provide specific and measurable targets:

1   *Elite targets*, for example, targets relating to a greater number of pupils achieving a *particularly desirable* target such as more with 5 A* grades at GCSE or achieving at Level 6 at the end of Key Stage 2.
2   *Average targets* such as a greater percentage of the year group achieving a recognised benchmark, e.g. Level 4 at the end of Key Stage 2. The DFEE's system is based on the setting by each school of average targets for each Key Stage.
3   *Reliability targets* such as a reduction in the number of pupils 'failing', for example that there should be no non-readers at age 7 or no children with no A*-C grades at GCSE.

Schools will need to decide whether to set targets of different types. If only average targets are used, this may lead to a lack of attention to the pupils at the upper and lower ends of the ability range. A mix of types will ensure that the challenge affects all pupils.

Challenging targets

In order to plan achievable but challenging targets, it will be necessary to benchmark against other schools. This process will need to take account of the differences and similarities between schools. For example, schools with a similar intake could be chosen, based on levels of free school meals, English as a second language and, for secondary schools, on selection procedures at the age of 11. This could, however, provide a minimalist rather than a challenging approach. Those schools who really wish to promote challenge and raise achievement will benchmark against other schools in the world, rather than against national or local norms. They will also consider what can be achieved using non-traditional approaches to learning. In some schools teachers have been setting targets for pupil achievement which are actually *behind* the pupil's current position (the historic zone in Figure 7.1). It is most important that information is used within the school to prevent this from happening. Targets which are set within the comfort zone are not especially challenging in themselves but may be appropriate if the pupils are tackling more challenging targets in other subjects. The smart zone represents the setting of targets which are challenging and where the school is trying to make a real difference in attainment. In order to ensure that targets are achievable, it is better to be realistic about capability and not to set too many targets in this zone. The 'unlikely' zone speaks for itself. Whilst 'wild' targets *can* be achieved under certain circumstances, failure can be very demoralising for pupils and staff.

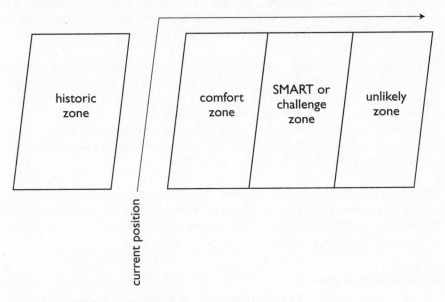

Figure 7.1 Progress towards targets.
Source: based on DFEE 1997b: 14.

Whose targets?

The importance of involvement in the operational target-setting process cannot be underestimated. Pupils will over-achieve on targets they set for themselves so their involvement is critical to success. A similar commitment can be gained by involving staff and other stakeholders in setting targets which apply to them. Nevertheless, schools and LEAs are under considerable pressure to contribute to the achievement of the national goals so there cannot be too much flexibility at the individual level.

The framework for an operational target-setting plan

In order to fulfil the criteria described above, we have devised an operational planning approach which has targets and plans at four interlinked levels:

- whole school targets and plan
- area targets and plans
- individual staff targets and plans
- individual pupil targets and action plans

The links are shown in Figure 7.2 below and we then outline our thinking in each of these areas.

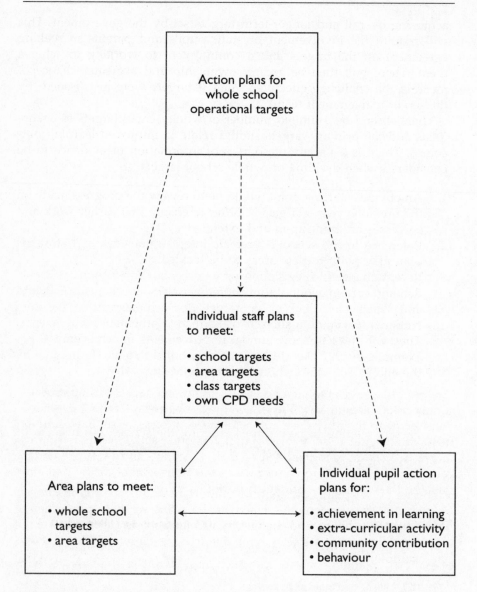

Figure 7.2 The types of operational target-setting plans.

The whole school targets

This process will be led by the school's senior staff and should involve a dialogue with other stakeholders as the targets are being determined. Schools will decide on targets for which they can take responsibility and which they feel can be achieved, while ensuring that they work towards achieving overall and longer-term targets set by the government. This will require the involvement of staff, pupils and parents in seeking agreement on the targets and a commitment to working to achieve them. There will then be greater ownership and a greater chance of meeting the challenge effectively than if targets were just 'issued' by the senior management team.

There should be a limited number of whole school targets to ensure focus and the primary targets should relate to improved learning outcomes. There is a variety of sources of information or evidence to be considered when deciding on whole school targets.

1 An obvious starting point would be to review the progress made on the previous year's targets in order to ensure that earlier work and successes are built upon and extended.
2 Reference to the school's strategic intent framework and strategic plan may point to new areas to be tackled.
3 Recent changes to legislation or to parental expectations will also demand certain action. From September 1998 all schools in England and Wales have had to set targets for achievement in the core National Curriculum subjects of English, Mathematics and Science. They will have to show annual improvements in achievement. For example, in 1997 David Blunkett set national targets, stating that by the end of 2002 the national tests should show that:

   • 75 per cent of all 11 year olds can reach Level 4 in maths
   • 80 per cent of all 11 year olds can reach Level 4 in English.

4 Factors relating to new pupils entering the school will need to be considered as they may have different prior attainment and needs to existing pupils.

Taberrer (1997) points out that it is important to link the *outcome targets* to the *processes* or activities listed in the plans so that approaches to learning and teaching and changes to management arrangements are not seen in isolation but are seen in relation to those targets. Table 7.1 shows an example.

Table 7.1 Linking outcomes and processes 1998/9

Outcome targets	Relevant process in the operational target-setting plan
add x to pupils' reading achievement tolerate no failure	e.g. daily reading hour train staff in high empowerment reading strategies strengthen and guarantee the home reading support

It is important to set up processes for reviewing the whole school targets. Some schools allocate the responsibility to a member of the SMT, often with a governor also taking an interest. In other schools, there can be a task force monitoring progress on each target. It is very important that a regular review takes place in order to confirm that progress is being made or to initiate remedial action.

The area targets

Each area of the school should demonstrate its contribution to the achievement of both its own and whole school targets. Schools will, by their very nature, have different types of internal organisation or grouping. For example, a primary school will probably do much of its standards-related target-setting based on achievement in National Curriculum subject areas for particular age ranges. Each year group or class will do further planning to achieve these targets and on topic plans. The school will need to decide which types of plans will be written in order to make the most effective use of teachers' time.

In a secondary school there will certainly be faculty and/or department plans but there will be a variety of other groupings depending on the way in which the school is organised. These may include cross-curricular aspects, houses, year groups, Key Stages and so on.

Each area will review its plans and targets for the previous year and will consider the needs of the whole school and its own development needs. It will then plan activities and targets in order to make its contribution to the achievement of whole school targets and its own needs. The area will have to decide who is responsible for ensuring that each target is implemented and will set up its own system of monitoring to ensure that progress is being made throughout the year. When the area plans are complete, they will then link to a key part of each member of staff's individual plan.

The individual staff targets

In the past there has been a very piecemeal approach to professional development for staff, especially for support staff. Schools which have been involved in the Investors in People initiative (or which have subscribed to its philosophy even though not seeking accreditation) have involved all staff in the vision, values and plans of the school and have shown commitment to professional development of all staff. For several years, all teaching staff have been involved in some form of appraisal but this has been pursued with varying degrees of commitment and, as originally conceived, almost disappeared in many schools. For a variety of reasons, the time is now right to rethink the approach to professional development for staff and the link between individuals and the achievement of school, area and pupil targets. The forces for change are:

- the introduction of the continuum of professional development for teachers by the TTA;
- the pressures from OFSTED to report on teacher effectiveness;
- the need to ensure that all staff are effective and providing value for money;
- the need to ensure that the appraisal of teachers impacts on pupil performance;
- the virtual disappearance of early retirement for teachers which means that many are left with an unexpected extra ten years of work with the consequent lack of career opportunities for those a decade younger;
- the government's focus on schools deciding and achieving overt performance targets.

The challenge is to find ways to empower staff to take responsibility for career development and salary management.

Each member of staff should demonstrate his/her role in achieving both whole school and area targets. Professional development targets will be set for each member of staff in order to support them in making this contribution and to assist them in developing their careers. Each member of staff will be linked to a mentor who will provide support in achieving the targets and will monitor progress. Similarly, each member of staff will contribute to the personal development of a group of pupils through providing support and monitoring progress. Thus, an individual member of staff is responsible for:

- contributing to meeting the whole school targets;
- making a major contribution to the meeting of area targets;
- implementing plans at the classroom level and monitoring pupil targets;
- taking responsibility for his/her own continuing professional development (CPD).

The individual pupil targets

Much work has been done in schools on the creation of Individual Education Plans for statemented pupils. In addition, many schools across the age range have put considerable effort into Records of Achievement so that pupils are encouraged to record their interests and achievements and to propose areas for action. Some secondary schools have worked with examination pupils (especially those at the

C/D grade boundary for GCSE!) in order to help them to work towards particular grade profiles. What is needed is a bringing together of these three initiatives and a partnership with parents so that each pupil is involved in setting some targets which provide a challenge. Although we include examples, there will be considerable differences for pupils across the age range and it may be valuable to involve pupils in the design of an appropriate proforma. Support and regular monitoring should ensure that each child is challenged to reach his/her full potential, both academically and in terms of involvement in a broad curricular and extra-curricular diet of activity. Barber (1996) develops the concept of the Individual Learning Promise as a means of ensuring that each pupil is challenged and supported.

Although the use of appropriate language would be important, the plan could include targets for:

- achievement in learning;
- extra-curricular activity;
- community contribution;
- behaviour.

In a secondary school, each pupil should be mentored by a member of staff who will offer support and monitor progress. This may be the class or form teacher or another appropriate person. In a primary school, the class teacher will have regular contact with the pupil and can offer support as needed.

The pupil targets will be linked to the whole school targets in a number of ways:

- whole school targets will be an aggregation of the individual targets;
- departments/areas will have to plan to deliver on the targets and will be accountable for their achievement;
- staff will take part in professional development activities in support of the targets
- management activities will be linked to pupil need, e.g. in ensuring resources for the provision of appropriate technology, well maintained premises, sporting facilities and staffing structures.

Proforma for an operational plan

Examples of completed proforma are included here. In Chapter 10 we produce blank proforma which the reader may wish to use or adapt.

Whole school plan (Tables 7.2 and 7.3)

The plan which is created needs to be sufficiently broad so as to apply across the school but it needs to contain specific and measurable targets and processes for ensuring that these are addressed by all areas of the school and are achieved within the time frame. The reviewer would normally be a member of the SMT.

Curricular area/key stage plans (Table 7.4)

The most important point here is to align area targets with whole school targets. Thus staff in charge of area plans should complete the proforma of how they are going to meet whole school targets before they fill in targets for the general development of the area. This is important if we are to avoid the failure of previous school development plans which merely aggregated individual area plans and did not create an overall organisational imperative. Although we have shown an example for a secondary school, we have not provided a primary example as schools will need to decide the extent and nature of any area plans e.g. by curricular area.

Individual staff action plans (Figures 7.3 and 7.4)

To avoid the 'wish list' approach of poor appraisal schemes, it is critical that staff are required to articulate how they contribute to whole school targets, area and class targets before defining individual needs. This will then bind them and make them accountable for organisational targets.

Individual pupil action plans (Figures 7.5 and 7.6)

The key purpose here is to engage pupils in taking responsibility for their own learning by articulating what they have to do to meet learning and other development targets.

Table 7.2 Whole school operational targets 1998/9: primary school example

	Target	Responsibility	Cost	Desired outcome	Completed by	Reviewed by
1.	80% of pupils in Year 5 to have a reading age at least as high as their chronological age	Jean Potter	£360–3 days supply Literacy resource boxes – £200	Active support of parents and use of literacy hour to ensure 80% reach the target in standardised tests.	July 1999	Matthew Taylor
			£1000	All staff to attend sessions on teaching literacy and follow-up with beginning action research project	March 1999	
2.	80% of pupils in Year 2 to reach Level 2 in maths; 20% to reach Level 3	Carol Parker	£120–1 day supply Time	Assess IT teaching in maths	May 1999	Susan Buchanan
				Training sessions in staff meetings		
			£240–4 half days	Effect monitored		
				More active teaching and use of IT and extension activities to ensure SATs results as per target.		
4.	Implement new system of monitoring progress in core subjects using software already in school	Peter Jones	£360 for supply to set up and support	Software on staff computer	January 1999	Matthew Taylor
				Forms in use		
				Training day		
				Data readily available when required from class teachers		
5.	Refurbish Year 6 area	Jean Potter	£1800	Decorated, furniture repaired, computer area with 6 sockets	April 1999	Susan Buchanan
6.	Increase display of work celebrating pupil achievement	Elaine West	£100	Opportunity for all pupils to have work displayed in a stimulating environment	December 1998	Susan Buchanan

The person with responsibility for a project will work with the various units in the school in order to produce a detailed plan for its achievement. There will be half-termly review meetings with the member of the SMT who is the reviewer for that particular target. Where appropriate, each of the units will include in its own plan the ways in which it will contribute to the whole school targets

Note: We have not attempted to provide the sub unit detail for a primary school. Schools will need to decide the extent to which more detailed breakdowns are needed, e.g. by curricular area or Key Stage.

Table 7.3 Whole school operational targets 1998/9: secondary school example

	Target	Responsibility	Cost	Desired outcome	Completed by	Reviewed by
1.	Improve levels of literacy	Kathryn Smith (Head of English)	£18000	70% of pupils in Year 9 to reach Level 5 in English	May 1999	Chris Moore
2.	Improve levels of numeracy	Barry Price (Head of Maths)	£15000	77% of pupils in Year 9 to reach Level 5 in Maths	May 1999	Lindsay Black
3.	Improve higher grade results at GCSE	Gill Davies (Head of KS4)	£10000	62% pupils to achieve 5 A*–C at GCSE	June 1999	Eric Goldswain
4.	Improve standards of teaching	Simon Jones (i/c staff development)	£5000	variety of styles used including IT, 90% lessons rated good or above	July 1999	Jan Hamilton
5.	Improve attendance in KS4	Lorna Crowther (HOY10)	£2000	electronic registration operating effectively; 97% attendance in Y10	November 1998 July 1999	Liz Poole

The person with responsibility for a project will work with the various units in the school in order to produce a detailed plan for its achievement. There will be half-termly review meetings with the member of the SMT who is the reviewer for that particular target. Each of the units will include in its own plan the ways in which it will contribute to the whole school targets.

Table 7.4 Curricular/area etc. plans e.g. for Science Department

PART I – TO MEET WHOLE SCHOOL TARGETS

Whole school target	Actions/tasks/strategies	Responsibility	Who involved	Cost (revenue and time)	Inset	Desired outcome (how know achieved?)	Completed by	Monitored by
1. Literacy – Y9	Creation of science dictionaries	Bill Desmond (i/c KS3 Science)	all staff	£100	2 hour meeting on training day	pupils understand meaning of words and can spell them – each has growing dictionary	July 1999	Jean Percy
2. Numeracy – Y9	Regular use of calculations	Bill Desmond	all staff	nil	normal planning time	calculations used at least once a month	in operation by November 1998	Jean Percy
3. GCSE results	Use existing data to set targets and mentor	Jane Hunter (i/c KS4 Science)	all staff	staffing for review time – £2000	1 day plus 2 hours for faculty	4 planned review points in Y11	October 1998	Jean Percy
4. Teaching quality	Peer review – varied styles, interest, differentiation and pace (further targets in this area next year)	Jean Percy (HOD)	all staff	staff time – 12 times 1 day i.e. £1500	2 hours on training day for peer review; pace and learning styles covered last year	all staff have observed 2 others and discussed styles	May 1999	Simon Jones
5. Attendance KS4	Monitor attendance and follow-up absence Ensure that lessons are interesting	Jane Hunter	all staff	normal procedures		Whole school systems implemented and utilised 90 per cent lessons rated good or above	January 1999	Lorna Crowther; Jean Percy

PART 2 – TO MEET AREA SPECIFIC TARGETS

Area-specific target	Actions/tasks/ strategies	Responsibility	Who involved	Cost (revenue and time)	Inset	Desired outcome (how know achieved?)	Completed by	Monitored by
1. Primary school links	Link with all 16 feeder schools to establish 'baselines' and basic certificate of competence	Bill Desmond	HOY 7 for coming year, HOKS3	£1000	£300 for one day visit of primary heads/ science co-ordinators	curriculum mapped, certificate system in place	April 1999	Jean Percy
2. Lower school health education	Review of PSHE and Science curriculum to identify overlaps and links	Bill Desmond	Head of KS3, HOY 7, 8, 9, plus 3 other staff	6 x 1 hour meetings	not Science budget	curriculum mapping complete	February 1999	Jean Percy
3. Incorporation of IT into lessons	Staff development, shadowing; equipment in all labs	Stuart Nuttall	all staff	£5000	time for shadowing, 5 1 hour workshops in directed time	each class using IT as a tool at least 6 times a year e.g. for control, measurement, calculation, display	July 1999	Jane Hunter
4. New gas and water taps	new fittings in S1–S4	Matthew Griffiths (technician)	–	£8000	–	fitting completed without disrupting lessons	March 1st 1999	Jean Percy
5. Improve staff Health and Safety awareness	1 day on H and S regulations; 1 day first aid course	Matthew Griffiths	all teaching and technician staff	£400	use training days	greater awareness of issues; 20% staff moving on to accredited courses e.g. First Aid at Work	February 1999	Jean Percy

INDIVIDUAL STAFF ACTION PLAN	
NAME *Carol Parker*	ACTION PLAN FOR PERIOD ......*Sept. 1998 to July 1999*......
YEAR GROUP *Year 2*	MENTOR *Matthew Taylor*

TARGET	ACTION PLANNED	BY WHEN?	COMMENT
More active teaching of maths and ICT extension initiatives	Visit B.J. School to see good practice		
	Assess current situation	Oct 31	
	Provide classroom support, monitor year group planning, key objectives, arrange staff meeting on extension activities,	December to May	
	Report to governors	June	
Develop parental links for reading	Workshop for parents	November 30th	
Own CPD	Complete masters degree based on numeracy project	June 15th	
	Attend one day course on the global classroom	November	

Targets should relate to   a relevant whole school issue
                             own CPD

Figure 7.3 Individual staff plans – primary.

INDIVIDUAL STAFF ACTION PLAN	
NAME *Bill Desmond*	ACTION PLAN FOR PERIOD ......*Sept. 1998 to July 1999*......
DEPARTMENT/YEAR GROUP *Science; Form tutor Year 8*	HEAD OF DEPT *Jane Percy*

TARGET	ACTION PLANNED	BY WHEN?	COMMENT
Whole school			
Manage introduction of science dictionaries	*Order materials, introduce to staff and monitor development*	*December 1st*	
Monitor and encourage use of calculations across science lessons in KS3	*Map across each topic and monitor pupil exercise books; produce worksheets*	*October 31st*	
Area			
Curriculum mapping of PSHE	*Draw up map of each area and highlight links and overlaps (work with SH)*	*April 15th*	
Pupil			
Achieve area target 1 – baseline assessment of Year 6	*Design or acquire instrument, introduce in each school*	*June 30th*	
Own CPD			
Advanced Professional Diploma in Enhancing the Learning Curriculum	*Attend evening sessions*	*May*	
First Aid at Work course	*Attend with colleagues in school and then follow up*	*July*	
Mentor a newly qualified teacher	*Work with senior teacher to develop skills*	*Sep–July*	

Targets should relate to   whole school targets
area targets
pupil targets
own CPD targets

Figure 7.4 Individual staff plans – secondary.

INDIVIDUAL PUPIL PERSONAL ACTION PLAN					
NAME Peter Duncan			ACTION PLAN FOR PERIOD ....Autumn 1999........		
CLASS Mrs Morrison					

What I would like to become better at	How do you think you could do this?	Who needs to help you?	What do you need to help you do this?	When will you do it by?	Teacher comment
In school:					
spelling	read more books	Mum Mrs Morrison	Reminders Quiet time	Christmas	*We will keep a chart*
8 times table	say it each day	Mum Mrs Robinson	Tests	November	*I will test you*
Out of school:					
score more goals	play for junior team go to holiday scheme	Dad my mates	team place and kit place at scheme	November	*See Mr Taylor*

Targets could relate to: achievement in learning
extra-curricular activity
behaviour

Figure 7.5 Pupil action plans – primary.

INDIVIDUAL PUPIL PERSONAL ACTION PLAN

NAME	ACTION PLAN FOR PERIOD
Rebecca Kemp	......Sept. 1998 to July 1999......
CLASS	CLASS TEACHER/PERSONAL TUTOR
9LP	Mrs Picktball

TARGET	ACTION PLANNED	BY WHEN?	COMMENT
Achievement in learning: improve homework marks – nothing below C/B	stay after school 2 days a week write at desk keep homework diary up-to-date	October 31st	A good plan
Extra-curricular activity: learn lifesaving join drama group	join classes on Saturdays join Tuesday lunchtime at school	October 1st joined both	See Mrs Hibbert
Community contribution: sponsored event for charity	organise for the class with 2 friends	February	We can plan this in PSHE
Behaviour: improve punctuality in mornings	set alarm no late marks	December 1st	Excellent idea

Targets should relate to: achievement in learning
extra-curricular activity
community contribution
behaviour

Figure 7.6 Pupil action plans – secondary.

References

Barber, M. (1996) *The Learning Game*, London: Gollancz.

Caldwell, B. J. and Spinks, J. M. (1992) *Leading the Self-managing School*, London: Falmer Press.

DFEE (1996) *Setting Targets to Raise Standards: A Survey of Good Practice*, London: DFEE.

DFEE (1997a) *Excellence in Schools*, London: HMSO.

DFEE (1997b) *From Targets to Action*, London: DFEE.

Ellison, L. and Davies, B. 'Planning in education management' in B. Davies, L. Ellison, A. Osborne and J. West-Burnham (1990) *Education Management for the 1990s*, Harlow: Longman.

Fullan, M. (1993) *Change Forces*, London: Falmer Press.

Office for Standards in Education (1994) *Improving Schools*, London: HMSO.

Taberrer, R. (1997) Lecture given to the Yorkshire and Humberside Region of BEMAS, Sheffield, 25 June.

Chapter 8

Operational target-setting
Primary school case example

Howard Kennedy, Holy Family
R. C. School, Berkshire

Holy Family School is set in an urban area on the edge of Slough, surrounded by two semi-council estates and a busy main thoroughfare into London. It is a two form entry primary school with 450 children on roll. There is a wide socio-economic mix of pupils. In 1996 the school had an intake two points below the national average (as determined by the Performance Indicators for Primary Schools). The school has been grant-maintained since 1992 and, subsequently, a Foundation School.

The school has been popular for a number of years and has been involved, as have many, in a wide array of initiatives designed to improve the quality of education which children receive. Standardised tests, development planning, improvement planning, assessment and evaluation have been constants in what has been a hive of activity. Visitors have been numerous, applications have soared, and in many ways we have congratulated ourselves on being committed, industrious and highly successful. There was, however, always a constant, gnawing doubt about the true and total effectiveness of all our efforts and how our leadership commitment to improvement actually affected the teaching and learning in the classroom.

We were effective in administering tests every year, in complying with external demands and in increasing significantly the amount of data collected, but we were singularly poor at investing enough time or expertise in analysing and using this information effectively. It is worth giving a record of our practice. It included: annual standardised tests in Years 2 to 6; SATs in Years 2 and 6; annual reports with National Curriculum levels; termly National Curriculum assessments (combined with regular provision of national curriculum levels when marking children's work); entry and exit assessments on every maths and science module. We also had an appraisal system which included pupil evaluation of teachers and curriculum delivery. We generated a lot of information but, in so doing, also created an environment of constant activity. It was this vast level of activity which became self-defeating for it militated against a reasoned, reflective atmosphere with enough time to evaluate initiatives properly. This is a very significant issue when one looks at the size of most primary schools and the lack of investment, with subsequent poor levels of staffing.

Reading Michael Fullan's book, *Change Forces* (1993) was a cathartic experience and a welcome boost to our confidence. Fullan identified that most educational reforms seldom achieved their objectives because they did not make a significant impact on the instructional activities of the classroom teacher. He also emphasised the enormity and the complexity of the challenges facing schools and teachers (Fullan 1993). This was a critical message which provided the impetus for us to review our practice and search for better and more significant ways to improve. There was a renewed determination to ensure that developments impacted on the classroom teacher.

This increasing awareness of the centrality of such thinking coincided with our decision to implement baseline assessment through the use of PIPS (Performance Indicators for Primary Schools, Durham University). This choice was made despite being under enormous pressure to adopt a different assessment system used by our LEA which linked to their formula funding. After much analysis, however, we chose to introduce a system which was best suited to our needs. The significance to school was that the PIPS scheme was simple to administer and time effective, as a child's individual test performance was sent to Durham University who then undertook all the detailed analyses, returning the information to school some six weeks later. This information is presented in a simple and easy to use format.

As in all schools, this process was taking place at the same time as a whole host of other activities, developments and initiatives. However, the format of the data from the baseline assessments was so simple to interpret that it had to be incorporated immediately. This was quite simply because the information provided was better than anything we had been able to produce in-house. It also illustrated, in a simple to understand format, that there were elements in the teachers' and individual children's performance which needed to be changed. Another major benefit was that the assessments identified some areas of outstanding success.

The school was responding to a professional drive to find ways of improving but, also, to an external environment which, increasingly, was demanding evidence of achievement and of improvement. Once the data had been received it seemed an obvious progression to discuss the content and issues with those teachers involved but also to involve the whole staff in examining the consequences of this new information. As a result of this experience, there was an increasing expertise in the analysis of data and a renewed respect for how it could be used to improve our whole school and the education of every individual child.

We decided that it would be sensible to revisit all the data we possessed and a detailed analysis was undertaken of our SATs results and standardised test scores as well as the Performance Indicators for Primary Schools. As a result of this, we decided to determine targets for individual teachers and year groups of children.

A group consisting of myself, two deputies and heads of Maths, Science and English worked on this task and quite quickly established global targets for each year group as shown in Table 8.1.

Table 8.1   Targets for the core subjects

Year 2	English	Maths	Science
Pupils reaching Level 2 or above on the National Curriculum SATs	90%	90%	90%
Year 5	English	Maths	
Pupils gaining above 100 on standardised tests	90%	90%	

However, before these were presented to the staff for discussion, they were radically altered as it was felt that such 'global' targets would not encourage best practice or cohesiveness and commitment among the staff. They would, we felt, create only winners and losers and ultimately this would be damaging to the school. We decided on a different approach whereby we set levels for *acceptable* and *outstanding* performance. We also resolved that to set targets at the top end of the range of ability would weight our approach to these children so we decided to set levels for our lower performing children as well as our most able. In effect, *bands of acceptable levels* of performance were introduced for each year, examples of which are shown in Table 8.2.

Similar bands were agreed with every year group and became our targets at the beginning of the school year. It is worth recording that Year 2 and 6 had targets for the National Curriculum SATs as well as standardised tests. As the end of the story, it would be good to report that everything had improved and we all lived happily ever after, but life in schools today is much more 'messy' than that!

'If we knew then what we know now' is a welcome reminder that change is not easy and you seldom get it right the first time. It was only in implementing such changes that we learnt from the process. For instance, we had set targets but little attention had been paid to budget decisions, time allocation for staff, curriculum time allocation for specific areas associated with our targets and the small issue of curriculum resources. In effect we had set off on this journey believing naively

Table 8.2 Performance targets for Year 6

Key Stage 2 Year 6		
1996/7 outstanding achievement targets	*1996/7 minimum acceptable levels of performance*	*1995 performance*
90% of year group to score Level 4 or above on SATs	80% of year group to score Level 4 or above on SATs	
Remaining 10% to score Level 3	8% to score Level 3 2% to score Level 2 or below	
25% to score Level 5 or above in English	15% to score Level 5 English	English 67% Level 4 or above
35% to score Level 5 in Maths	20% to score Level 5 Maths	Maths 72% Level 4 or above
		Science 69% Level 4 or above

that if we did what we had always done but also set targets, then performance would improve. Target-setting by itself does not work: probably worse, it creates failure. Targets beware!

That is probably the most important part of this chapter for anyone involved in primary education and is recognition that there are no easy, ready-made panaceas which can be transposed onto a school to provide instant and outstanding success in every area. Purkey and Novak (1996) talk about the importance of 'stories' and 'journeys' and it was only as we progressed on our journey that we learnt many of the lessons which, ideally, should have been known at the beginning.

Throughout this school development, I was becoming the archetypal 'frantic learner' (Pollard 1997) with a keen interest in understanding how children learn and, thus, how we could improve our school. This led into reading recent publications about the brain and a discovery of the enormous amount which had been learnt in the last ten years about the psychology of learning. This became an exciting pursuit and a new language entered the school: Brain Gym, brain breaks, optimal learning conditions, Neuro-linguistic programming, visual, auditory and kinaesthetic learning, music therapy, multiple intelligences, memory techniques, alpha, theta, delta, beta brain waves and the value of relaxation. These discoveries were tremendously exciting but a great challenge to the teaching and learning styles and curriculum delivery throughout the school.

We had organised a training day with a consultant on Accelerated Learning and this proved to be the most powerful stimulus to change that I had ever witnessed in a group of people. We all took part in the most stimulating, interactive day which enabled us to understand the value of new approaches to our teaching and to children's learning. It was a day of revelation but also the day when our training needs were firmly cemented to our organisational aims. I, as the headteacher and lead learner, was suddenly surrounded by staff who had also become committed 'learners'. The 'learning school' was developing and the environment was altering significantly. There was a renewed sense of excitement and energy as all our expectations of children's potential had been challenged. There was a feeling among many that it was no longer children who failed school but schools which failed children and that the notion of a 'below average' child was erroneous.

Area meetings (teams of teachers working with more than one year group such as, for example, Early Years) were held with myself and critical issues arose, some of which were seemingly impossible to solve in mid-year. Resource issues were relatively simple although computer technology, which was a significant part of the developing culture, was a seemingly insurmountable obstacle. Much more difficult was the issue of time: time allocated to each area of the curriculum and time available for staff to meet the myriad demands in an effective manner. Issues were sufficiently important to necessitate radical solutions so the timetable was re-organised in mid-year, a 'teaching of reading' half an hour was introduced on a daily basis, more structure was applied to the content of all our English lessons, an agreed common approach to the teaching of maths lessons was initiated, based on Anita Straker's National Numeracy Project, and there was the voluntary introduction of brain compatible teaching strategies. Things were changing, a fact which always reminded me of a quote by Dr. Patrick Porter:

> If you continue to think what you have always thought, you will continue to get what you have always got!
>
> (Porter 1993: 117)

As this 'moving school' (Stoll and Fink 1996) progressed, our school-based training ascended to an impressively high level, with staff designing and providing the most demanding, challenging, but hugely enjoyable sessions, totally in accord with their new found knowledge about brain compatible learning. The method became the message and educated and reinforced our development. Before the reader gives up, thinking that life had suddenly become blissful for all, it hadn't. It was as 'messy' as ever but there was a renewed enthusiasm emanating from me and replicated in varying levels by all the staff. We had learnt, again, that teachers enjoy things that work in the classroom.

Out of all our activity arose an 'acquaintance' with the work of Bob Slavin in America and the concept of 'Success for All' entered our thoughts. The same message had been 'writ loud' in all the brain material so this became a natural addition and development to our thinking and thus were laid the seeds of our present 'Total Success' target. This was a significant development as it altered our thinking regarding the importance of value-added measurement and increased our commitment to absolute targets. We began to realise that our school improvement and development would include both these types of measurement.

We were learning from our experiences and it was evident that budget decisions had to be made for the future so that significant resources could be allocated to support the achievement of our main purpose. This would mean a radical change in the structure of some elements of the school which would mean that there would be some turbulence ahead. We had begun to understand that decisions would be based on the analysis of data, so our first investment would be to get our mathematician to spend time on this task. He analysed all the standardised tests and SATs information and Durham University provided detailed analysis of our Year 1, 2 and 4 performance.

We then spent a day with our staff looking at these results and reflecting on all the activities of the school. It many ways this was the dawning of a new era in that we decided on three main targets for the immediate future: one for children, one for parents and one for staff. This meant that we had only *one target* for improving standards in the school which was a radical departure from the numerous targets of previous years. It was a pretty impressive target though: '*total success*' in reading within three years. In practical terms 'total success' would be measured with the expectation that every child would have a standardised reading score above 100. As the 'average' range in such tests is usually 90–110 our target of 100 meant we were aiming for a mid-point of average for every child in the school. Such a statement is relatively easy to write down but we spent three months analysing the many implications of such a decision.

One of the central elements for this three month period was a determination not to proceed until we had the commitment of 100 per cent of the staff. This 100 per cent commitment took three more evening sessions and one whole day to attain, as we worked through every aspect and consequence of the implementation. In many ways, this reflected the perceived Japanese decision-making process where all the issues and problems were identified and solved before the decision was taken. Our English co-ordinator, Melanie Wheeler, included a significant element in every meeting and that was to ask the staff at the end of each session to place their 'name tags' on the appropriate column indicating their disposition: 'total commitment', 'committed' or 'against'. It took two months to get everyone into the 'totally committed' column and this is now displayed in our staffroom for everyone to see on a daily basis.

This was an illustration of a major change in our thinking and approach to our second year of target-setting which was primarily to spend as much time as was needed before making the decision. It was essential that all staff were in agreement and that every reason and excuse had been removed before we started on what was obviously going to be a tough journey. Throughout this process another significant development was taking place and that was a development in the vocabulary and language of the school. The power and effect of language should not be underestimated, nor should its value in any reform programme.

> All my life, I assumed that somebody, somewhere knew the answer to the problem. I thought politicians knew what had to be done, but refused to do it out of politics and greed. But now I know that nobody knows the answer. Not us, not them, not anybody.
>
> (Senge 1990: 281)

The analysis of data and our whole school commitment to 'total success' had a range of consequences which impinged on every aspect of school activity. The PIPS data provided us with information which showed the annual rate of progress of individual children, whole class and year group as measured against the national average. This gave us the opportunity of analysing teacher performance which initiated discussion about success and failure and the need to consolidate and change. It also provided ample information to design individual and year group 'value-added' targets.

The data analyses had shown some interesting aspects, two of which are worth illustrating. Our PIPS data appeared to show that experienced teachers had much better results than more recently qualified teachers and that this latter group seemed to perform at an acceptable level in the middle ability range at the expense of those children at the extremes of the ability spectrum. The second major discovery was that results in Year 2 and 6 were higher than other year groups, which we concluded was a reflection that these two age groups had their results published for parents and, in the case of Year 6, for national league tables. Other year groups had no such external accountability. Whilst we recognise that to make decisions based on such data is fraught with difficulties, we have always made decisions in the past and now we felt this information was helping our decision-making process to be more effective.

This led to changes in the organisation of the school and the beginnings of our own action research projects. The latter deserves an initial 'health warning' for practitioners and needs a short illustration of our local, inadequate approach to this development, in that our first efforts would not stand up to the scrutiny of any researcher, which is perhaps an inherent danger in allowing schools, in isolation, to make their own conclusions regarding data analysis. We recognise this is a very sensitive area and one which needs careful monitoring. We are excited, however, at the prospect of becoming much more focused in our curriculum design and delivery and feel we are becoming more effective through the use of data analysis.

As a result of our work, we determined that the four new staff arriving in September would all be placed so that they were working in a collaborative and co-operative way with an experienced member of staff and would be part of an experienced 'team'. We also initiated a new classroom arrangement for our Year 2 children, in that a highly successful teacher agreed to have a class made up of both the most and least able children, leaving her two newly appointed colleagues with children in the middle range. Although the effect of this change will not be properly known until the June PIPS assessments, already there have been significant developments which were identified as a result of other actions taken for our 'Total Success' literacy programme. This year group was assessed six weeks into the term as part of a process of identifying focus groups in need of special attention for literacy. The large majority of children identified were in the two new teachers' classes and the experienced teacher with the lowest performing children had a much lower number who qualified. The discovery of such occurrences is indicative of our new data-driven approach and a reflection of a much more analytical means of improvement.

We knew that decisions would be needed for support staff and that time would be required for the implementation of any planned activities, so provision was made in our budget planning and funds were earmarked for this school improvement activity. We also recognised a need to increase our knowledge and expertise regarding the teaching of literacy and reading and engaged the help of one of our country's leading researchers on this subject, Dr Greg Brooks, and spent an enthralling day at the National Foundation for Educational Research examining similar, although on a much larger scale, reform programmes around the world. His expert knowledge was a huge bonus and helped us to realise that there are no 'off the shelf' solutions but that there are successful ingredients in all reforms. We determined to implement the successful elements of these programmes in designing our own approach.

Staff meetings and training sessions took place at every stage of development and finally, a fully comprehensive plan was agreed. This transformed our Teaching Assistants into a Task Force with weekly training sessions and daily contribution to the 'targeted children'. These children were selected for the programme after analysis of previous performance and on a new reading test. The 'Literacy Hour' was already in place although ours extended to one hour and 20 minutes each day, with 30 minutes dedicated to the teaching of reading. This latter development required attention for all our staff as the demands this made on their expertise and knowledge were significant and this was identified as an issue for whole staff training.

Letters and advertisements were posted throughout our community and 'any offers of help' were welcomed. These included non-employed parents, the retired and an occasional shift worker. The English co-ordinator needed time to meet all these groups, to gain their commitment and understanding of the requirements, to organise a timetable for their involvement and to negotiate their entry into school with the class teacher. Our list of volunteers stands presently at 28.

Each child on the programme was to receive focused teaching on literacy three times daily. This involved new practices with IT and the introduction of numerous literacy-focused games. Each child should have a fourth daily offering and this would take place at home with parents agreeing to this commitment. For those for whom this was not possible, a homework club would be established.

School-based action research projects were to be established, looking into the effectiveness of Neuro-linguistic programming on self esteem and spelling and Brain Gym on self esteem, literacy and numeracy. In the first instance, these would be monitored through 'soft' indicators but, during the course of the year, a more empirical research-based project was established as part of the headteacher's Lincoln University International MBA programme. Older pupils were also to be involved in the programme as 'paired' mentors to younger children who were in the 'focus groups'. Child and parent attitude surveys are planned as part of the evaluation of the project.

Another exciting development was the identification of Optimal Learning Environments through the personal research of our language co-ordinator. As she became immersed in brain-based research, she presented the staff with an interesting discussion document relating to the numerous elements which should be present if there are to be optimum conditions present for children to have the best opportunities to learn. A list of points illustrates the extent of the discussion and indicates many agenda items for future development: availability of water to drink, music, furniture, posture, lighting, peripheral messages, signs and symbols, air quality, exercise, passive/active learning, temperature, humour, novelty, games, aromas. Such a list might create scepticism in education but is one which numerous companies and industries have long since seen as an essential environment for high-performing individuals.

The project manager would obviously require time to monitor and support all the people involved in the programme and this required budget provision as did the flexibility to enlist the help of external expertise to work with all the staff and the need to send staff on appropriate external training courses.

The changing environment within the school was being data-driven and we arrived at a point where new targets were designed for all children and for the whole school. This had two elements. The first was the creation of an absolute target in literacy with every child in the school reaching a standardised score of above 100 within three years. In effect this means that the school has set itself the interesting challenge of getting every child, in reading, beyond the mid point of average. As we are already within the early days of this process, it may well be that the timescale and the absolute target need reviewing. It is, however, essential that it is recognised that, through this very demanding process, all our previously held expectations are re-examined and a big effort is made to discover whether such an achievement is possible. Reading, initial experience, the help of an external linguistic expert and brain-based research suggest that it is possible.

There is also a worthwhile human reason for us to pursue this challenge – the pupil. On one occasion, I was reviewing targets with two teachers and they were happy to settle on a 15 per cent 'failure' rate. At this point I asked them to put names to these 'failures' and then to imagine that their parents were observing the conversation. This was not quite blackmail but an interesting experience and one which motivates committed teachers to reassess their own beliefs. Reviewed targets were also established with every teacher which were an improvement on the previous year for two good reasons: the environment of the school was changing and the need to illustrate improvement was accepted by all and the data provided by PIPS was a significant improvement on anything that we had previously. This latter development suddenly enabled us to identify targets on an individual as well as class and year group basis.

Developments do not take place in isolation and, as our school became immersed in new discoveries about teaching and learning, an environment of innovation was gradually being created where some staff were willing to question previous beliefs and practices and were 'having a go' at new initiatives. Interestingly such consequences, whilst in some ways increasing pressure, were better and more positively received because they focused on children, their learning and improvement. They are still a source of excitement for some but a challenge for others. We have learnt that in any reform programme there is a full spectrum of response and performance. However, as we had learnt from other initiatives, it was the process of change as much as the intended outcomes which was crucial to the success of any programme and we were creating an environment where teachers and children were learning together and change was seen as a natural consequence of activity.

Times, however, had changed. Change by itself was no longer sufficient and empirical data was demanded to demonstrate improvement. For this reason a structure of regular assessment was critical. Reading tests were introduced every half term and, crucially, these were to be internally 'published' so that progress was transparent and any evaluation could take place in an atmosphere of openness and honesty, tough as this might be for individuals where progress was not evident. This was critical if we were to learn from failure as much as from success. In this way, data was to be regularly collected and analysed and conclusions integrated into future activities. Such an environment encourages teachers to analyse what works and what is less successful and, it is to be hoped, encourages a sense of collective growth where all in the school are committed to improving performance and attainment. The primary school of the future will no longer be a haven for ineffective teachers, and those performing at a less than acceptable level will only remain if they show a commitment to their own development and improvement and can 'evidence' such developments through pupil attainment.

The first year of our global targets saw improvement in many, but not all, areas of the school, although the Year 6 SATs showed significant increases:

Year 6 SATs 1996	Year 6 SATs 1997
Maths 72% level 4 or above	Maths 92% level 4 or above
English 67% level 4 or above	English 78% level 4 or above
Science 69% level 4 or above	Science 88% level 4 or above

Such figures have to be treated with caution as the tests from year to year have no correlation. However we would like to think that the children had improved owing to the decisions made regarding curriculum time allocation, resources, focusing on individual needs, improved teaching, improved assessment procedures, pupil involvement in target-setting, improved learning techniques, curriculum design and the subsequent change in the 'climate' of the classroom. It is worth stating that the children and testing procedures were externally monitored by NFER in 1997.

The whole process is extremely demanding and our experience suggests that schools need to focus on one main target for improvement because even one element is incredibly complex as this summary illustrates:

Table 8.3 Summary

	Challenge	Effect
Leadership: whoever is leading at any particular stage	Search for improvement Lead learner Extend personal knowledge Change personal expectations Work towards evolution of new goal Lead, inspire, motivate, educate Change language of institution	'Frantic learner' Heightened personal motivation, satisfaction, enjoyment, challenge Increased activity
Decision-making process	Need to involve all those whom decision will affect Need to 'internalise' for all those involved Close to total commitment	Needs large investment of time Need management skills to lead individuals, group/s Provides focus Training needed in Decision Thinking Data driven
Budget	Plan in advance Allocate sufficient human and financial resources Skills audit Appoint appropriate staff	Finance Committee involvement 'Educate' Finance Committee Invest to improve mentality required Need good information, theory, research and evidence if available
Management	Ensuring necessary procedures are in place Include monitoring and evaluation as part of the process Redesign roles and responsibilities e.g. Teaching Assistants	Increased skills required Data-driven decisions Classroom reorganisation Staff allocation Inexperienced staff paired with experienced

Environment	All need to become learners Language must evolve and change Innovation to be encouraged and failure tolerated 'No blame' culture 'Total success' culture 'There are no excuses'	Excitement, enthusiasm, fear, turbulence, resentment, focus, schisms, challenge, development, change as a constant Requires leadership and management
Curriculum	Time audit Reorganisation New elements introduced Rationalise total provision	Pressure More initiatives New elements provide new challenge Teachers need to increase expertise
Teaching	If I can't do all I've always done what can I do? Find new and better ways Intellectual growth, search for meaning	Challenge, excitement, fear, enthusiasm, focus, anger Pressure More learning More work Change Turbulence
Learning	New experiences for children Monitoring and evaluation measures efficacy Evolves as teachers increase expertise Classroom environment changes Action research projects initiated	Excitement, enthusiasm, increase in active learning More movement Increased pupil involvement in learning Greater dialogue between teachers Sharing of experiences Parental enquiries Children 'paired' with others and become part of teaching
Language	New language provides challenge for all All need encouragement to participate, increase personal understanding of and use new terminology	Affects culture Requires open and honest environment to encourage personal growth Apprehension Language precedes growth so time is required for all to 'internalise'

Governors	Need to inform and provide regular communications Allay fears and promote positives Increase understanding Focus on achievement and improvement Workshops and evidence	Excitement, fear, change Lack of interest by some More initiatives Doubt League tables Requests for information, evidence
Parents	To inform and provide regular communications New language for parents Need to educate and improve knowledge Assuage any fears and promote positives	Parental enquiries Intrigue, fear Appreciation and especially so as they see improvement in child's performance Requests for opportunity to increase their own knowledge Increased community involvement
Children	Involvement in target-setting for group and individual 'Paired' partners	Increased commitment Focus Greater dialogue between pupil and teacher Greater motivation
Teaching staff	Initiative fatigue Questions existing practices and beliefs More change Higher levels of performance Increasing personal knowledge, skills and expertise Time Sharing 'teaching' of 'their' class children with others Increased profile of Teaching Assistants Publication of personal results	Need for teachers' 'lifestyles' to be reviewed, monitored and kept in 'good health' Time for reading and intellectual development required Periods of stability required Turbulence associated with change Increased anxiety at increased expectations Increased rewards as success becomes evident

School-based training	Focus on target Reflects new pedagogical beliefs New learning for all staff	Excitement, enthusiasm Increased professional motivation based on success of new approaches Increased impact on classroom practice Identification of need for all to become learners in new environment

These developments are improving the quality of education that we are providing for our children and improving the efficiency and effectiveness of the school and its teachers. If there were simple solutions, however, schools would have adopted them many years ago and the project outlined has many serious consequences and questions to answer. Target-setting may well improve schools but it is driven by the assessment procedures and it is these procedures which have a huge impact on the type of education that our children receive. It is so easy to be seduced into assessing only those things which are easily assessed and, as such, to provide children with a very narrow, and often passive, style of education. Our experience has produced many reservations about the type of education that our children are receiving. PIPS, SATs and Standardised Tests provide information about some aspects of children's intellectual development but there are numerous important elements of a child's growth which are totally ignored: emotional intelligence, multiple intelligences, problem-solving, the ability to work with others and thinking skills. We should all be committed to improving standards of achievement but we must also remain committed to those elements which we feel will improve all our children's life chances.

The reform illustrated above arose as a natural development of our first attempt and wish to improve the education that we gave our children. It has had many positive effects on the school and on individual people. The headteacher and an increasing number of staff have changed their attitudes and beliefs concerning the ability of all children, regardless of initial levels of performance, to achieve an average or better level. This is no easy task and perhaps the first requirement in setting out to achieve it is to create an environment which is built on the premise that the more we know the more we need to know, for we need to search still further afield to find more and better solutions. This implies that we accept change as an inevitable consequence of progress and that everyone in the school is a 'learner'.

We know from initial results that a number of our New Learning

Technologies have huge potential and we can recognise that much more of children's learning must be matched to their individual learning styles. We have reinforced a belief that there are no easy solutions but that working through co-operative and collaborative structures is a rewarding and successful way to approach our future. We understand that structure and systems are crucial to any effective reform programme and we recognise that data analysis informs budget decisions. It is also understood that there is a cost for any development and that monies diverted from one source have a direct consequence on other activities.

We are grateful that we had the wisdom to focus on only one Target for Achievement and Improvement, for we realised that this singular task was incredibly complex and demanding. And, without doubt, this has proved to be the case. We have come to realise that in many ways the focus on literacy and reading is semi-irrelevant, for the whole process is one of reviewing the pedagogical skills and effectiveness of the individual teacher in the classroom in order to improve the learning attainments of every child and that the knowledge and skills learnt through this process can be transferred to every area of the curriculum. As a consequence every person in the school must be a 'learner' and schools must be as much about learning for adults as for children.

While the process is extremely demanding and seemingly never ending, we can gain some support from the words of Michael Fullan who writes that, 'Aside from religion, teaching and learning is as close to the meaning of life as one can get'(1993: 145).

References

Fullan, M. (1993) *Change Forces*, London: Falmer Press.

Pollard, W. (1997) 'The leader who serves' in F. Hesselbein and R. Beckhard (eds), *The Leader of the Future*, San Francisco: Jossey Bass.

Porter, P. (1993) *Awaken the Genius*, Phoenix, Ariz.: Purelight Publishing.

Purkey, W. W. and Novak, J. M. (1996) *Inviting School Success*, Belmont Calif.: Wadsworth Publishing Co.

Senge, P. (1990) *The Fifth Discipline*, New York: Doubleday.

Stoll, L. and Fink, D. (1996) *Changing our Schools*, Buckingham: Open University Press.

Chapter 9

Operational target-setting
Secondary school case example

Sue Cowans and David Jones,
The Philip Morant School, Colchester

The Philip Morant School is an urban comprehensive school which shares a campus with two very successful selective schools and a Roman Catholic secondary school. Our intake, therefore, has a considerable gap at the top of the ability range but the average score on intake is usually around 100. For some years the percentage of pupils achieving 5 or more A*–C grades at GCSE has been around 65 per cent. Five years ago we began looking at target-setting as a means of school improvement and with the immediate goal of breaking through the 70 per cent 5+ A*–C barrier. In the summer of 1997 we achieved the figure of 73 per cent 5+ A*–C grades. In order to achieve such success and to realise our over-arching aim, which is to enable students to develop to their fullest academic potential, it is important that all staff understand, and work in unison on, a whole school policy of target-setting. If the targets are to be instrumental in moving forward learning and teaching, they need to be set after consideration of the following criteria and with reference to the school's aims and its plan:

- Thoughtful planning must take place to ascertain what is a reasonable and attainable target, both in terms of timescale and required progress, for individuals and groups, by subject and cross-curricular area.
- It must be clear by whom and for whom the target is set. The performance criteria against which success will be measured must be identified in the initial stages of planning.
- In order to set the next target a review will be necessary of the previous stage so that it is clearly understood what has brought about the starting point or baseline for the next stage.
- There must be careful thought given to strategies to bring about the required changes that will lead to meeting set targets. Learning objectives will have to be identified and a scheme of work developed that will enable progress to occur. 'Pastoral' support systems will also be important.

- Interim reviews will be necessary, to check that progress is taking place and to identify obstructions to progress.
- The work scheme may have to be modified if the original plan is not leading towards the target.

If this process is to become integrated into learning and teaching across the whole school, it will be important to create a positive ethos to this approach and to make sure that all staff are trained to become confident in target-setting. The collection and presentation of assessment data, vital to establishing baselines and against which realistic targets can be set, needs to be done in a way that allows the school to be 'rich' in data but not drowned by it. The collection of assessment data needs to take place efficiently, so that it serves and informs learning and teaching, and is not seen as a burdensome task that overcomes the important outcomes that must be achieved. Effective use of ICT and secretarial support should allow all teachers access to useful data. This, in turn, should give teachers a clearer picture of students' strengths and weaknesses and allow planning to be more focused and differentiated, avoiding repetition or gaps in study.

Sharing this information in a sensitive and positive way with students and parents is important in raising expectations, but also avoids the frustration of uncertain or unrealistic targets. A mixture of negotiation and directive are required to give the targets rigour and a healthy level of tension is what provides the motivation and incentive to keep the process moving forwards. An historical perspective on what has been achieved within the school and a lateral view of what has been possible in similar organisations nationally helps to co-ordinate the target-setting.

In essence, the development of a target-setting process is simply formalising and making more overt that which has always been inherent in good teaching practice. In doing so, it allows all staff and students access to higher achievement and reduces the risk of students underachieving through lack of awareness, or underestimation, of the potential that is there.

Whose targets?

Target-setting in this school takes various forms and is applied to individuals, groups and the school as a whole.

- *Pupils* in the lower school are set formal targets following the process of self evaluation and consultation with their tutor. Their targets are usually about work in class or a more constructive approach to homework. These targets are written up in their personal planners and are reviewed twice a year. Pupils in the

Upper School do this in the form of expected grades for GCSE, A
levels and GNVQs.

- *Staff* are given information about the potential of their pupils from
  Year 7 onwards. During Years 10 and 11 they are given targets for
  their teaching sets which relate to the overall targets of the faculty.
  Following examinations they are given feedback on their teaching
  groups as to how individual pupils performed in their subject with
  reference to the average score for all their other subjects. This data
  is supplemented by national data based on YELLIS (see Box 9.2)
  feedback. (The same process is repeated using ALIS data (see Box
  9.3) data for Years 12–13.)

- *Faculties* are given targets for expected results at Key Stage 3 and
  Key Stage 4 and at 18+ examinations. Heads of Faculty are
  expected to break these down for individual teachers. A great
  deal of targeting goes on for borderline groups of pupils who are
  identified approximately twelve months before the examinations.

- *Whole school* targets are set in relation to NFER CATs data (see Box
  9.1), YELLIS and ALIS. For example the percentage of pupils
  achieving an average CATs score of 95+ is a very reliable indicator
  of the number of pupils likely to achieve 5 A*–C grades at GCSE
  level. To discover this was, for us, like finding 'The Holy Grail'.
  How does a school really know what its overall targets should be?
  These figures have given us targets stretching over several years
  which suggest that we should be achieving around 73–75 per cent
  5+ A*–C grades.

Types of tests and targets

The school had a history of using *cognitive abilities tests*, with the particular focus of detecting students with special needs across the whole
ability range. There have always been compensatory programmes for
students with particular learning difficulties and also Extra Studies for
very able students and those with high levels of ability in particular
areas. As one way of identifying these students, along with recommendations from staff, the tests had proved to be a useful and accurate
source of information. Until about four years ago, all feeder primary
schools had conducted standardised tests, the scores of which became
available to us on transfer into Year 7. With the introduction of Key Stage
2 testing, this practice had ceased and initially anyway, the Key Stage 2
data has not appeared to be sufficiently diagnostic as baseline data. We
decided to re-introduce CATs tests for all Year 7, after students have had
a few weeks to settle into our school. These are conducted in a positive
and non-threatening manner. We feel these are a good indicator of
performance across a wide range of abilities and match those tested at

GCSE. In this context, we were encouraged by the results of a large-scale project examining the predictive value of the CATs in relation to GCSE results carried out by NFER. This work will be useful to us in forecasting realistic targets for our students and will give a national perspective against which to set targets.

Box 9.1

CATs – Cognitive Abilities Tests (NFER – Test D)
These standardised tests are completed in September of Year 7 and act as a baseline measurement of three strands of ability: non-verbal, verbal and quantitative. This profile of each student is useful in the process of drawing up Year 7 teaching groups into two broad bands of ability and the regular monitoring of this to ensure that student placements are correct. This process will be further enhanced by the tests from now on being done in Year 6, with the support of our primary colleagues. CATs continue to be useful throughout Key Stages 3 and 4 as a baseline measure against which to monitor progress and as a predictor of GCSE performance in our target-setting. The extensive research carried out by the National Foundation for Educational Research (NFER) into the value of CATs as predictors of GCSE performance and our own research over a series of years to investigate the correlation between non-verbal scores and GCSE results gives us confidence to use these as a measure of 'minimum expected targets' for GCSE.

Having been involved in *Key Stage 3 tests* from the early pilot days, we are now beginning to see trends emerging that may be very useful in our work. Our involvement with David Jesson's work at the University of Sheffield and his final report on the reasonable correlation between Key Stages 3 and 4 are of great interest to us in our further work.

YELLIS allows us to gain a quick 'snapshot' of our students' performance in abilities that correlate with GCSE performance. It also gives us a vital national perspective on our students' 'chances' at GCSE, by plotting their results against a much larger national survey of achievement than we could achieve if only monitoring our own performance. The use of *ALIS* in the sixth form is also important for the same reasons.

Box 9.2

YELLIS (Year 11 Information System)
This data is available to us through our enrolment into the extensive research project conducted at the Universities of Durham and
Newcastle. All students complete two tests (mathematics and vocabulary) and a questionnaire in Year 10. The results are processed to
place students into one of four bands A to D. 'Chances graphs' are
provided to give indicators of potential student performance within
these bands in a wide range of GCSE subjects. These are derived
from a large-scale sample of past performance, as the GCSE results
of project schools are collected each year and used to correlate
YELLIS bands against GCSE outcomes. The questionnaires collect
data on students' own aspirations and have been useful to us in
identifying and 'action planning' with students who have low
aspirations for their own future educational plans. After our
GCSE results have been analysed, the school receives feedback on
the performance of each department within the school measured
against each other, to give a positive or negative 'residual'. The
GCSE performance of our students by subject is also compared
with similar students in other schools to produce residuals for
each subject department. This can be seen as the 'value-added'
measure of each department in the school.

Box 9.3

ALIS (A Level Information Systems)
ALIS produces data on student intake characteristics such as
gender, ethnicity, home background, prior achievement (GCSEs)
and ability (International Test of Developed Abilities) score) in a
way which allows each institution to compare its students with
all others in the scheme. The A level results are adjusted to take
account of student intake characteristics so that institutions can
compare their own students with a similar group of students in
other participating institutions.

Throughout the history of the school, the summative performance of its
students at GCSE has been analysed. With the use of information
technology, this is now an easier process and results, converted into
scores, can be used for many different analyses. Individual student
profiles, departmental profiles and teaching set profiles can be drawn

and residuals calculated between individual and average performance. These are used to identify the different levels of performance and to seek answers to these differences. If this analysis is used in a positive way, it encourages good and successful practice to be shared within and across departments. Also it builds a model of performance that will in time give greater accuracy to the target-setting that is such an important part of the process of raising achievement. Student performance is monitored in this way at three points:

- June exams in Year 10;
- October interim report grades in Year 11;
- Mock grades in January of Year 11.

A retrospective review carried out in September, after the results, analyses the performance of the whole school, departments and individual teachers and students in their performance outcomes at the end of Key Stage 4. The aim of this is to improve performance in the next learning cycle by identifying areas of strength and weakness to inform planning of the next stage.

The target-setting process

The school recognises as fundamental to its aims the importance of academic achievement. We are aware of the multiplicity of factors that play a part in this, beyond measurable baseline achievement. Many of these can be described as of a qualitative nature and are impossible to quantify. Many are particular to individual students and may be beyond our control, such as the level of home support, emotional difficulties and many other socio-economic factors. We are, naturally, also concerned with the development of the 'whole student' and see academic performance as only one facet of this. We have countless systems to foster the many other valuable assets of personality that we hope all our students will develop in their time with us. We do believe, however, that one of our main duties to all our students and their parents is to enable them to develop to their fullest academic potential. It would be too late if we uncovered academic under-achievement only as they reached the terminal stages of their formal education programme with us. Therefore the fundamental aim of the process outlined here is to raise achievement in academic performance throughout Key Stages 3 and 4 and into our sixth form programmes of study. The data collection and analysis described in the following sections is, therefore not to be viewed as an 'exact science', but as an aid to assist teachers and students in monitoring performance, as part of our focus on constantly improving the quality of our learning and teaching strategies.

All targets are set annually and reviewed mid-year. The Head and SMT are responsible for setting overall quantifiable academic targets for the end of Key Stages taking account of baseline assessment, national targets and prior school achievement. The targets are written into the school plan. The assessment manager develops methods for data collection and presents it in a way that is accessible to all staff and gives training in its use. Heads of faculty/department interpret these targets into subject and teaching set targets and also write schemes of work that will ensure that the targets can be met. Subject teachers interpret group targets into individual targets for students. They ensure that the scheme of work can be delivered in a differentiated way and monitor the progress of individual students towards their targets. Heads of house, tutors and academic counsellors are involved in the review of targets at year, tutor group and individual level. Targets are recorded in student planners and on reports to parents.

The process involves the input of data into spreadsheets (in our case, Microsoft Excel) which can then be analysed in a number of ways and presented in a variety of forms:

1 Baseline data at the beginning of Key Stage 3 and 4 (Key Stage 2 levels, CATs scores, Reading scores, NFER D and E, Key Stage 3 levels):

   - to assist with the banding and setting of pupils;
   - to identify the distribution of ability across the year group;
   - to make comparison with the national distribution of ability;
   - to set realistic targets for the future (Key Stage 3 and 4 expected outcomes);
   - to act as a benchmark in the detection of underperformance.

2 Termly Assessment Sheets:

   - to monitor individual progress in attainment and effort on agreed whole school criteria;
   - to detect underperformance;
   - to act as a discussion document for academic counselling;
   - to assist in the monitoring of placements within the ability bands.

3 'GCSE' scores throughout Key Stage 4:

   - to monitor attainment against CATs, Key Stage 3 tests and YELLIS tests;
   - to monitor attainment against effort to detect underperformance;

- to set realistic targets to motivate students and departments and individual teachers;
- to monitor performance within and between subjects;
- to improve modelling of school performance over a period of years.

Key issues

There are a number of key issues which contribute to the success of the system. Data must be accessible to all teaching staff and it is presented and explained to heads of department and heads of house by the assessment manager to ensure consistency in its interpretation. The 'sensitive' nature of the data is fully discussed to ensure its use in a positive and constructive way. Targets set are 'realistic minimums' to avoid demotivation in less able pupils. Paper copies of targets are stored in departmental files, allowing instant access and monitoring of achievement by all teaching staff.

Long-term profiles can be developed across Key Stages 3 and 4 and into the sixth form. School performance can be monitored year on year. Department and individual teacher group performance can be monitored year on year. Profiling allows closer monitoring to take place within academic and pastoral contexts and facilitates bridging between these two key areas.

Benchmarking is carried out through the use of the following:

- LEA data
- National data
- School's historical data
- YELLIS and ALIS feedback on the actual results PICSI profile (see Box 9.4)

Box 9.4

PICSI (Pre-Inspection Context and School Indicator) report
This provides detailed reports of schools about to undergo an OFSTED inspection. In particular there is a detailed analysis of the school's position in relation to other schools in the area and nationally. It also puts the school in its social and economic context. It looks at results from the aspect of gender and also provides information as to how various departments and subject areas are performing compared with other departments in the school and departments in other schools.

Conclusion

Our system provides all staff and students with a regular review of progress. This enables under-performance to be identified and remedial action to be taken before it is too late. Having achieved our early goals by the use of these methods, we are more than ever convinced of the need to set both students and individual teachers challenging but realistic targets. We are currently working on the link between Key Stage 3 test results and GCSE results. From this preliminary work, one set of statistics is quite startling:

1994   % of students achieving an average of Level 5 or above at Key Stage 3 was 67%

1996   % of students achieving 5+ A*–C grades at GCSE was 67%

Chapter 10

The new model

A framework for schools

In this chapter we bring together the components of the planning process which we have described in this book, with cross-references to the appropriate chapters where each part is explained in more detail and exemplified. After the last of these proformas, we demonstrate how the various processes might be integrated. We suggest that the school plan should have five sections as follows:

Section One   A brief outline of the school
Section Two   An outline of the school's futures perspective
Section Three   The strategic intent
Section Four   The strategic plan
Section Five   The operational target-setting plans

Section One: a brief outline of the school

This would explain:

- the school's values;
- its core purposes;
- basic data: (i) location;
              (ii) type;
              (iii) pupil roll, groupings, ages, etc.;
              (iv) staffing structure, number and roles.

We would see this as being no more than two or three sides of A4.

Section Two: An outline of the school's futures perspective

The school should articulate any results of the futures thinking process (as discussed in Chapter 3). This can be done either in text form or by using the following proforma.

Future aspect identified	Potential impact on the school	School response
1.		
2.		
3.		
4.		
5.		

Figure 10.1 Proforma for the school's futures perspective.

Section Three: The strategic intent

The formulation of a strategic intent is described in Chapters 4 and 6. As well as the textual explanation, the following proforma can be used.

Intent	Capability-building measures	Move to strategic plan OR / Reformulate intent

Figure 10.2 Proforma for the school's strategic intent.

An example of a completed proforma can be found on page 115.

Section Four: The strategic plan

The development of this proforma is described in Chapters 4 and 6. An example of the completed proforma can be found on pages 112–113.

Strategic planning area	Strategic planning activities	Time frame	Responsibility	Cost
The learning outcomes: pupil progress & achievement				
Support for the quality of learning & teaching processes				
Management arrangements: physical & financial resources, school structure & organisation				

Figure 10.3 Proforma for the school's strategic plan.

Section Five: The operational target-setting plans

The school will need to highlight and articulate its key targets and activities for the following 12 to 24 months. This will need to be broken down by the use of several proforma. We show in Figures 10.4 to 10.8 some of the proforma which might be used. They cover the whole school plan, the curricular/area plans, the individual staff plans and the pupil plans (as described in Chapter 7).

Target	Responsibility	Cost	Desired outcome	Completed by	Reviewed by
1.					
2.					
3.					
4.					

Figure 10.4 Proforma for the whole school operational target-setting plan.

Whole school target	Actions/tasks/ strategies	Responsibility	Who involved	Cost (revenue and time)	Inset	Desired outcome (how know achieved?)	Completed by	Monitored by
1.								
2.								
3.								
4.								
5.								

Figure 10.5a Proforma for curricular/area plans: part 1 – to meet whole school targets.

Area specific target	Actions/tasks/ strategies	Responsibility	Who involved	Cost (revenue and time)	Inset	Desired outcome (how know achieved?)	Completed by	Monitored by
1.								
2.								
3.								
4.								
5.								

Figure 10.5b Proforma for curricular/area plans: part 2 – to meet area specific targets.

INDIVIDUAL STAFF ACTION PLAN

NAME	ACTION PLAN FOR PERIOD
	....
DEPARTMENT/YEAR GROUP	HEAD OF DEPT/MENTOR

TARGET	ACTION PLANNED	BY WHEN?	COMMENT

Targets should relate to   whole school issue/target
area target
pupil targets
own CPD targets

Figure 10.6 Proforma for individual staff plans.

INDIVIDUAL PUPIL PERSONAL ACTION PLAN

NAME	ACTION PLAN FOR PERIOD
	....
CLASS	

What I would like to become better at	How do you think you could do this?	Who needs to help you?	What do you need to help you do this?	When will you do it by?	Teacher comment

Targets could relate to: achievement in learning
extra-curricular activity
behaviour

Figure 10.7 Proforma for pupil action plans – primary.

INDIVIDUAL PUPIL PERSONAL ACTION PLAN

NAME	ACTION PLAN FOR PERIOD ....
CLASS	CLASS TEACHER/ PERSONAL TUTOR

TARGET	ACTION PLANNED	BY WHEN?	COMMENT

Targets should relate to: achievement in learning
extra-curricular activity
community contribution
behaviour

Figure 10.8 Proforma for pupil action plans – secondary.

The integrated nature of the plan

We have, in this chapter, shown the various components of the plan but, as the reader will recall, the original diagram shows that practitioners in schools will be working at all three strands concurrently.

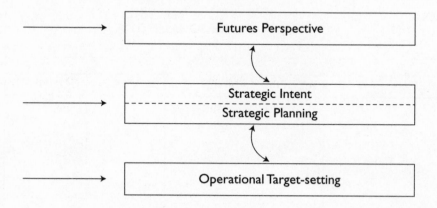

However, a mental model may be useful to highlight this integrated nature and a set of linked cogs, as follows, provides this model.

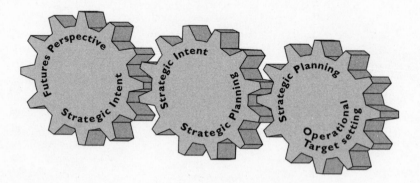

In the companion volume to this book we will examine in depth the process elements of planning now that the new framework has been established.

Chapter 11

Interpreting the new model

Robert Gwynne, Principal of
Longsands College, Cambridgeshire

This chapter is in four parts. First, by looking at the recent history of development planning at Longsands College the reader can see where the school has come from and then second, a critique of that experience is offered. Third, the chapter then reshapes current practice into the model proposed in this book. In the final section, I look at how the college will undertake the next round of planning (beyond 2000) using the new model.

Background and current practice

Longsands is a large (1500 students, aged 11–18) comprehensive community college situated in a market town which is close to Cambridge and near enough to London to be a dormitory for commuters. It has always been regarded as a successful school but six years ago, following my appointment as Principal, the governors and staff recognised the need for re-focusing and a new strategic direction. Also, at that time, the performance culture was just beginning to bite and there was a real need to improve examination results, intake levels and parental satisfaction. Viewed with hindsight, we embarked on a multi-track journey aimed at improving performance, raising quality standards and increasing effectiveness. All three of these themes have sound academic traditions and we fed off these in working forward.

Six years later the college is a very different place. It has shed its complacency and become a good and developing school. Much of this success is attributable to the strategic planning processes which we used. These reflect the accrued professional and academic wisdom on this theme. However, whereas they were useful tools, we now need new procedures and ways of thinking to take us forward again. The twin reasons for this are the limitations of current planning methods and the fact that 'conventional' processes are now implicit and subconscious; we now need new vehicles. These points will be developed as I proceed with this case study.

Three distinct phases, spanning the last six years, can be identified. The first is what existed when I inherited the college leadership. The second covers a three-year period when most existing practice was questioned, destabilised and replaced with often *ad hoc* arrangements. The third covers a period in which new structures and procedures have been installed, tried and used to achieve clear strategic goals. Running through the period has been an implicit desire to develop a sense of educative leadership, participative action and staff development. The process has been assisted by a significant level of staff turnover, arising from promotions and retirements, and the recruitment of staff who are 'of a like mind'.

The college had been run very successfully for many years on a 'top down' model which my predecessor described as 'running like a Swiss watch' – and indeed it did. However there were very few expressed long-term goals and little or no articulation of strategic intent. The emphasis was on maintenance activities and opportunist developments such as TVEI. Development plans did exist but they were cumbersome documents that were not understood by staff or seen as part of their routine existence. Development planning was something to be done to satisfy the requirements of the school or external bureaucracy.

The first task, and the beginnings of the second phase, was symbolised by the creation of the Mission Statement. Although the final wording is my own, the compilation was a collective activity involving all teachers (at the creative stage) and governors (at the ratification and refinement stage). This was the first educative and involving act and teachers relished the opportunity to have their voices heard. The resulting statement enshrines over 40 key concepts and is expressed in just over 100 words. The aim was to produce an enduring statement that would condition and shape all future actions by determining a framework of values and educational intent which characterised the college's future.

> Longsands is an outward and forward-looking college, which exists at the heart of the local community. We aim to work closely with our partners to achieve success and quality in all our endeavours. We seek to achieve this by:
>
> offering broad and balanced educational, recreational and social opportunities for people of all ages;
>
> giving equal value to all college members irrespective of ability, gender, race or creed;
>
> recognising that each person has individual needs and must be helped to achieve appropriate types of success;

encouraging students, staff and governors to expect the best of themselves and others at all times;

providing an orderly, secure and pleasant environment in which hard work, enjoyment, mutual respect and care for others are of paramount importance.

There then followed two end-on 'strategic plans' which were simply lists of things which needed to be done. They were designed through the usual process of brainstorming, classification and target-setting. Whereas they had a sense of direction, it could not be claimed that they were driven by a particular structural view of the future. Their purpose was to review and replace existing ways of doing things in line with the general feel of the new mission statement. Examples of key points for action in these early plans included the redesign of school uniform and the revision of the Key Stage 3 curriculum plan. A lot of necessary metaphorical cupboard clearing, furniture moving and replacement went on. At this stage the big new strength was staff involvement and experimentation in collaborative ways of working. Staff found this both liberating and educative as well as, in some cases, threatening and destabilising. All the certainties of yesteryear were evaporating and this included 'knowing where one stood'. Many decision-making structures were *ad hoc* and this lead, quite reasonably and deliberately, to discussion about the nature of shared power. Cynics argued that it was a wolf in sheep's clothing; others relished a sense of involvement and self-actualisation.

Three years on a new sense of frustration began to emerge. Staff began to question the *ad hoc* approach to decision-making and began to thirst for a clear set of goals for future development. This was a major achievement. Such articulation would not have been possible at the start and now a huge appetite for involvement existed. Recognising this, I decided to take stock and to establish a new set of goals that fitted into a 'futures' view of the college and its work. The analysis began by me interviewing every member of the campus staff (over 150) to ascertain their perspective on what we had achieved and where we should go next. A summary of the findings was written and circulated. Other evidence in the form of parental and student survey findings was amassed and analysed. Also, we reviewed demographic and finance information to complete the backcloth for our new strategic plan which was to be called 'Towards 2000'.

The governors debated the best approach to quality management and decided on the OFSTED approach in preference to alternatives such as ISO 9000 and Investors in People. The new plan was therefore framed in terms of the OFSTED elements such as 'quality of teaching' and 'quality of learning'. Also, the time had come to install into the college a new set of management and decision-making arrangements which reflected both the philosophy and practice that we had been working towards in the last three years.

The new framework of goals was designed to fit in with a new model for involving staff in discussion and decision-making. The College Management Forum (CMF), comprising all team leaders, had been formed three years earlier but with an imprecise brief. Now it was to be used as the umbrella organisation for eight areas of college goal development. These were:

Campus development	Finance development
Community development	College-wide issues
Curriculum development	Pastoral development
Staff development	Performance development

Each area is serviced by a small number of CMF members who meet as a group charged with development work on everybody's behalf. The whole forum discusses proposals and the senior team takes executive decisions and actions.

'Towards 2000' identifies key goals under each heading and these have their origins in the evidence accrued during the research phase outlined above. There are between four and six goals for each key area. Some goals are quantitative and highly specific. For instance, a key goal in the Performance section is 'The College will strive to achieve a position where its GCSE results are about 10% above national averages.'

Other goals are qualitative and more generalised. An example of this comes from the Pastoral section: 'We shall continue to strive to find ways of involving parents in their children's learning and performance'.

A commentary referencing each key goal section to the OFSTED quality framework is also provided as a reference point. An example of this occurs in the campus development section under the heading 'Implications for the Quality of Learning' where it states: 'Poor quality buildings are often associated with poor learning. The demands of the National Curriculum suggest the need for high quality provision'.

For each key goal area and for each operational team (e.g. department or year team) there is a two-year development plan, which sets out the actions to be taken in pursuit of the key goals. In these plans reference is made to the specific objectives, timescales for action, budget implications, staff development implications and evaluation procedures.

The three governors' sub-committees each had a responsibility for two or three goal areas. This provided the final link in the chain and the role of governors as monitors and critical friends with a non-executive interest in the proceedings was established.

The overall model looks like this:

Mission Statement   *leads to:*
Key goals in eight areas   *leads to:*
Team level action plans of three types: Key goal areas
                                          Subject plans
                                          Whole college aspects

A first evaluation of this way of working was our OFSTED inspection in 1997, nearly three years into the life of the plan. It provided reassurance that the way of working was bearing fruit and evidence of considerable success in achieving our goals. What the inspection could not provide was a critique of the methodology. The OFSTED framework is blindly obedient to the conventional wisdom of development planning and regards development planning as an essential tool. This places a strait-jacket over the potentially liberating impact of development planning. So we were faced with the need to produce our own critique of our methods and their successes and weaknesses.

A critique of the Longsands approach

There is nothing startlingly radical about the college's approach. It could be regarded as 'good solid stuff' that does the job of providing a stable and clear platform from which the college can move forward. Similarly, it gives us a vehicle from which we can evaluate our performance and achievements.

The relationship between the plan, in the form of key goal areas, and the organisational furniture used for managing change provides a valuable symmetry. This has made it relatively straightforward to locate bits of the action into particular individuals' or groups' terms of reference. Herein lies a potential weakness. Locating key goals into operational structures almost certainly means that all goals are perceived at an operational level. The model, because of this functionalism, does not distinguish (at least at goal level) between futures thinking, strategic intent and operational goals. To the user of the plan, teachers, leaders and governors, it is a conveniently classified list of action points providing clear guidance on issues to be tackled. It does not provide a hierarchy ranging from 'sometime in the future' to the 'here and now'. In many ways the vision remains concealed and the reader has to interpret and read between the lines to get a feel for the college's destiny.

A real strength however, has been the impact of 'Towards 2000' on staff and governors. The process has enabled many stakeholders to become involved and to have their point of view recognised. Through involvement, their own understanding and skill level has been enhanced. This has materialised as a 'lingua franca' through which negotiation and discussion takes place. The existence of reference points provides certainty and removes ambiguity. It also provides points of accountability for leaders and followers alike. Simplicity and clear pathways give a reassuring and straightforward approach to development planning which staff and governors like and respect.

Another key point is the recognition that planning of this type is a necessary stage in the evolution of the organisation. It is as if we had to go through this stage before moving to a higher form of planning. In so doing, what has gone before becomes implicit and becomes the fuel for a more enlightened or appropriate approach next time around. It is interesting to note that ten years ago rudimentary development planning techniques needed to be taught to team leaders in schools and made very explicit. It is now the case that the basics are implicit and can be assumed. Whereas it was once essential to write down every element, a lot can now be taken for granted. The window is therefore open for an approach that can seriously impact on school reeningeering.

Reshaping current practice into the new model

As schools 'convert' from the widely accepted way of development planning into the new framework, we need to look at what can be salvaged from the previous approach. There is little point in starting from scratch simply for the sake of it. The purpose of this section is to look at the existing Longsands plan ('Towards 2000') and to re-orientate it into the proposed format.

Many of the steps outlined in earlier chapters were undertaken during the construction of 'Towards 2000' and this will be true for a lot of schools. Key points of similarity are:

- some attempt was made to look into the future;
- efforts were made to understand local trends and developments;
- the changing educational climate was acknowledged;
- economic pressures were recognised and efforts made to take these into account;
- the consumer element was taken account of by recognising the outcomes of surveys;
- account was taken, intuitively, of the college's position on the Sigmoid curve.

A key difference is one of emphasis and systematic analysis. In the new model, far more time would be put into the preparatory analysis before the goal-setting process starts. In the case of Longsands it could appear that the analysis of context is used to rationalise the chosen goals, rather than determine them. In reshaping our practice we would need to be far more rigorous in our contextual analysis.

Attempts to change mind-sets did not feature in the preparatory phase. The emphasis during the staff interviews was on 'How do we become better at what we have already elected to be?', rather than 'What do you think lies beyond the wall and into the future?' Staff were not asked to crystal ball gaze and to speculate on the future world our students would inhabit. It could be argued that this had already been done when, three years earlier, we produced our new mission statement. In part, this was the case but the mission statement is more about values than speculation on the future. Values have an enduring quality and do not change significantly even if we 'go over the wall' and into the future. They provide the bedrock within which futures thinking should be set. We speculated on the climate and ethos which we wanted but not on the skills, concepts and knowledge that our students would require, or the kind of world that we would be living in.

At least, we tried! The critical difference between what we achieved and what is proposed in this book is one of orientation. To help understand this we need to focus on the outcome of the planning exercise, that is – the goals. The Longsands plan has 47 key goals expressed in the following categories:

Overarching general goals   4

Campus development	6	Finance development	5
Community development	6	College wide issues	7
Curriculum development	6	Pastoral development	4
Staff development	5	Performance development	6

No further sub-classification is made in the plan, nor is it evident to the reader. The plan can be regarded has having a linear or 'horizontal' orientation rather than a 'vertical' one. Each horizontal aspect is further elongated by the existence of related operational targets as expressed in some or all of the action plans. The goals and action lists are functional devices for managing change. In terms of the Davies and Ellison model, 'Towards 2000' does not distinguish between futures perspectives, strategic intent, strategic plan and operational target-setting.

However, all is not lost because it is possible to re-orientate the existing goals into the new framework. This helps us to see how balanced the outcome really is. One would speculate that the majority of the goals would fall into the operational target-setting class. Analysis, however, reveals the following:

'Towards 2000' goal classification	Total number of goals	Futures perspectives	Strategic intent	Strategic plan	Operational target-setting
Overarching goals	4		2		2
Campus goals	6		1	2	1
Community goals	6	1	2	2	1
Curriculum goals	6		3	2	1
Staff development goals	5		2	3	
Finance goals	5		2	2	1
College-wide issues	7			7	
Pastoral goals	4		3	1	
Performance goals	6	1	2	1	2

Figure 11.1 Analysis of Longsands key goals ('Towards 2000') by new model type.

We conclude that 'Towards 2000' is strong on strategic intent and planning but noticeably weak in terms of overt futures thinking. The analysis is salutary. The strategic/operational emphasis is further compounded if the action plans, with the heavy emphasis on operational goals, are added to the picture.

Two questions arise at this stage. Firstly, do we have an overt futures perspective or is it implicit, as suggested earlier? Secondly, how important is it for us to articulate the futures perspective and can it be expressed as 'goals' in the accepted sense?

Chapter 3 suggests ten areas for examination in futures thinking and also offers a method for analysis. This would have been useful but the outcome would not be expressed in terms of goals; it would be a position statement. Perhaps this is why few of the 'Towards 2000' goals have a futures feel to them. I conclude, therefore, that the plan would be all the better for a futures section situated after the part dealing with accrued evidence, planning factors and planning parameters and before the sections outlining the key goals. Inevitably, the existence of the futures section would have changed some of the goals that were set.

A factor to consider here is the relationship between this discussion and the position of the school on the Sigmoid curve. When 'Towards 2000' was produced, Longsands was on the 'steep uphill' part of the curve. Arguably this is precisely the point at which a futures perspective is needed. However, pragmatism and short-term considerations tend to dominate. This is an indication of a particular mind-set often evident in schools. It works on the basis that by resolving all the outstanding issues we can then move onto considerations of the future. Unfortunately this way of thinking is a strait-jacket and can lead to inappropriate and wasteful action.

If we think now of re-packaging the contents and underpinning thinking into a framework compatible with the model in this book, the following picture emerges. This approach keeps us safely in the comfort zone. It helps reader-practitioners to see how their existing efforts can be utilised as a halfway house before embarking on a radical re-think at the next appropriate point in their school's development.

Transferring 'Towards 2000' into the new model changes the contents page in the following way:

	Original Version Contents	New Version Contents
Introduction	inspirational comment and preface from Chairman of Governors and Principal	as before but reference to futures thinking
Mission Statement	restatement of the background and its importance	emphasise values and enduring qualities as distinct from futures thinking
The first Strategic Plan	review of past work and achievements	as left
Creating the new Strategic Plan	outline of process	as left
The evidence	evidence from surveys and interviews	as left
Planning factors	local and national trends	as left
Planning parameters	future demographic and financial data	as left
Futures analysis		NEW SECTION which makes full use of data in the previous 2 sections, plus commentary and discussion
The Key Goals	as described earlier, in eight sections	as before, but a new classification introduced to provide details of 'type' e.g. strategic intent or operational goal

The point of this illustration is to indicate the relative ease with which an existing plan can be converted to assimilate the broad principles of the model. Other schools using other formats could easily undertake a similar conversion, thus bringing their existing way of thinking closer to the new model. The school then becomes better equipped for a new approach 'next time around'.

This conversion is, of course, fairly simplistic and ignores the radical effect which comprehensive futures thinking would have on the selection of key goals. It has also not addressed the need to make similar conversions to the operational plans that exist at team level. This latter point may not be too problematic as most action points in such plans are firmly pitched at the operational target-setting level anyway. In the new model they are likely to continue to exist in this form. The point remains, however, that key goals determined through a full futures thinking exercise may well be different from those arising from the current process.

In this section little or no attention has been given, so far, to the difference between strategic intent and strategic planning. It has been assumed that the existing key goals can be sorted, where they have a strategic dimension, into the two types. For this purpose, the key difference (assuming the goal is a strategic one by definition) is whether or not the goal is immediately actionable. If it is, then it can enter the plan and be prioritised accordingly. If a degree of developmental understanding and re-orientation is required, it must stay at the level of strategic intent until such times as it becomes sufficiently understood to begin work on. Two examples, chosen from the 11–18 section of the existing 'Towards 2000' goals are:

STRATEGIC INTENT:	STRATEGIC PLAN:
'Emphasis will be placed on developing differentiating learning programmes and courses suitable for all abilities.'	'The college will implement post-Dearing curriculum changes in Key Stages 3 and 4.'

No mention is made in 'Towards 2000' of timescale or the order in which the various goals will be worked on. This is deliberate and would remain so in the re-worked version. The reason for this is that the operational plan is a different document. Currently, at Longsands, the operational element is contained in the team level action plan documents and also the implementation booklet ('Towards 2000 part 2'). In re-configuring the plan it is unlikely that anything would change. Futures thinking and strategic intent items will seldom, if ever, have timescales attached. Strategic plan items and operational goals can, and should, be scheduled. This is the case in the current model and is the subject of discussion in Chapters 6 and 7.

The concept of 'readiness' is often used at Longsands in connection with futures matters and strategic intent. We have often found that an idea or intention has to achieve a 'critical mass' before it can be usefully and productively translated into an action. The factors determining critical mass are varied but include such aspects as:

- attitudinal matters;
- timing;
- reactive needs – such as public relations aspects or marketing;
- changes in personnel;
- finance.

Thus an idea may well be kept on hold for some time and then, because circumstances become right, it can be activated and moved rapidly up the list of priorities. This phenomenon exemplifies why futures thinking and the integrated approach to development planning are so powerful. Futures thinking, adequately expressed, and lists of strategic intents, provide continuous reminder lists that can be acted upon when the time is right. To not do this work often leads to important parts of the jigsaw becoming overlooked.

In summary, this section has illustrated how an existing development plan can be reworked to bring it into line with the new model. The next section describes how, armed with the Davies and Ellison model, Longsands will go about producing its next strategic plan 'Beyond 2000'.

Constructing 'Beyond 2000'

By now the reader is familiar with many aspects of the Longsands planning document, 'Towards 2000', which has been used as a case study for considering new ways of planning in secondary schools. We now turn our attention to the future and consider how we would construct the successor plan which we shall call 'Beyond 2000'. The aim is to allow the reader to reflect on how one school would blend its existing traditions and practices with the new proposals. This will help schools to create their own pathways for future planning.

This is one leader's perspective of how it could be done and it is not claimed to be the only way. Each school must work out its own solution, bearing in mind that the starting points will be different. Also, it is important to note that this section of the case study is at risk of repeating earlier chapters. Hence, some of the methods and procedures have been changed or adapted to illustrate, again, how one school could do the job.

We do not start with a clean slate and recognition of 'where the school is at' is an important starting point. Several features emerge at the beginning of the exercise that condition the pathway thereafter. Again, in this illustration, these are relevant to Longsands only but each school will have a certain number of 'givens'. These reflect the history and recent development of the school. They concern the managerial and leadership culture rather than educational matters. They set the scene and are the benign enablers. The following list applies to Longsands; brief descriptors are given to help the reader interpret the factor:

- The micro-political climate of the school
  usually positive and supportive, can become a problem when the institution is under pressure or facing major change.

- The decision-making and consultative apparatus
  well established and working well (as described earlier); it is important that this remains undisturbed.

- The leadership values
  aim to be educative, supportive and inspirational; well-understood
  and significant 'comfort' factors; could be a problem if there is a
  change in leadership in the near future.

- The nature and style of interpersonal relationships
  constructive and friendly; good sense of common purpose and staff
  enjoy working at the school.

- The development level of the staff
  a high level has been achieved which enables all staff to work with
  complex new ideas.

- The readiness of the school to embrace complex new thinking
  a clear test will be: 'will it benefit the students?'

- The language of previous development planning
  is well understood (e.g. key goals) and should be retained wherever
  possible.

This analysis is important because it helps to identify both the structures
and values that will be carried forward. Some schools, where work on
this front is less advanced, will wish to use the new plan as an opportunity to reposition the management and leadership furniture. The decision at Longsands would be to carry forward and build upon existing
arrangements, taking into account the vulnerable points identified
during the analysis.

The following features would therefore stay in place and need to be
taken account of:

- The College Management Forum (CMF) organisation and the
  development groups would stay in place;
- The decision-making method would remain basically as now,
  possibly with some shift towards executive power on the part of
  CMF groups;
- The links to governors sub-committees would stay but be
  strengthened;
- The college mission statement is unlikely to change (it being more
  to do with enduring values than with futures objectives);
- The notion of key goals would stay as an essential part of the
  vocabulary and planning process.

The next important step would be the evaluation and catalogue of
progress during the period of 'Towards 2000'. The resulting position

statement, like the context statement discussed above, would provide an important foundation for building the new plan. At this stage it is important to engage all the stakeholders both those who have an interest in recent progress and those who will be affected by the new plan. My preferred method for conducting this evaluation would be to commission an external review with very clear terms of reference. This work is time-consuming, but unlike OFSTED inspections, non-threatening. Considerable time, on the part of the evaluator would be spent analysing available evidence and talking with individuals and small groups in a semi-structured way. The resulting report would need to be brief and easily digestible. It would form an overview of recent achievements. Chapter 5 of this book contains some indication of techniques that could be employed for this purpose.

My preference for an external evaluator is a pragmatic one. This task needs doing thoroughly and is time-consuming. It also requires particular skills and an objectivity that may not be available 'in-house'. The evaluator must be capable of rapidly assimilating the culture, health and achievements of the school. Similarly, the capacity to abstract and synthesise from a wide range of sources will be an essential quality.

Caution and clarity are necessary at this point. This step is not about identifying future directions; this comes later. It concerns the building up of a position picture and analysis of what has been achieved. It needs to have an inspirational as well as a critical dimension. A sense of celebration must be one outcome, as this is very important for motivational purposes.

With this step complete, work on the preparatory phase of the new plan can begin. Earlier chapters provide methods and techniques that can be employed at various stages. In terms of Longsands, I envisage three types of 'building' activities.

The first will be to establish a futures thinking group with a brief to provide a futures perspective for the new plan. It will be a short-term issue group constructed for the purpose and with a membership drawn from all the identified stakeholder groups. Care and attention will be taken to draw in people with an appropriate disposition and notice will be taken of the 'right brain/left brain' notions outlined in Chapter 3 of this book. The group will not exceed ten in number, will be expected to complete its work in a given period of (say) a month and would be chaired by me. An essential part of the work would be some external stimulus inputs both about educational developments and about parallel exercises in other organisations.

The second building activity will be the assembling of relevant data. This would take four forms:

- opinion data from stakeholder groups such as parents, students, and the community, most likely provided by surveys;
- financial information on current and future budget positions;
- market information and demographic trends;
- educational performance data, trends and expectations both locally and national.

The third element will be a revisit of a tried and tested method at the college. That is, a personal interview with me for every member of the college staff and governor using a set of questions given in advance. The merit of this is that it gives first hand impressions of where people are and what they perceive to be the future needs. It can be claimed that this is not objective, as people will simply tell me what I wish to hear. Previous experience and a high level of trust (a payoff from investment in staff relationships) suggest the opposite and it is one of the few first hand opportunities the leader has for real opinion gathering.

There then follows the huge exercise of goal identification based on all the accrued evidence. At this stage the planning exercise would become the province of the senior team, possibly taking place in an extended off-site working session. The first step will be the refining and summarising of the futures statement. It will be done in such a way as to ensure that it becomes a major influence in identifying goals (remember that the futures thinking does not, in itself produce goals, although it may imply goals for either the intent or plan stage).

Thereafter, the work can move into identifying key goals from the sources of evidence that are now at hand. As goals are identified they would be classified into the eight operational areas concomitant with the CMF organisation and also (and here is the big new step) according to whether they are matters of strategic intent, strategic plan or operational objective. Similarly, appropriate timescales and methods of achievement would be attached. Later, at a refining stage, cost implications, staff development implications, monitoring and evaluation techniques will be ascribed. A conditioning feature of the exercise will be to ensure that around 40 key goals are identified. Careful scrutiny will be used to ensure that both the wording and intent of the key goals ensure they can be appropriately located in the new model.

A first draft of the new document will then be available for scrutiny by staff and governors as part of a final checking operation. The purpose of this will be to enable gaps, omissions or contradictions to be spotted by a wider audience. In all probability the contents list will be the same as the one suggested earlier.

The next step would be the construction of operational plans to support the key goal sections. This work would proceed as before and take place at team level but using different proforma styles to indicate much more tightly the linkage to the key goals and the contribution that each team level action would contribute to the overall plan.

The presentation of each page of the document dealing with a key goal area would include the following sections:

Title of page	key goal area; e.g. 11–18 curriculum.
Commentary	outlining and reminding the reader what the futures thinking statement said about this key goal area.
Key Goals: Strategic Intent	numbered goals (three or four) which cover the strategic intent for this key goal area expressed in the terms suggested earlier.
Key Goals: Strategic Plan	numbered goals, (three or four) which form part of the strategic plan with suggested timescales.
Operational Goals	specific targets to be achieved in given timescales; these are identified from the key goals

The plan would thus shape up and the whole booklet, including the prefacing contextual information and futures statement would constitute about 20 pages.

'Beyond 2000' will thus provide a clear platform for the college to operate on for the next planning period. This is likely to be about four years.

The benefits of this process and the outcome are in keeping with those suggested throughout this book. The plan will be a coherent expression of intent that is based on two main foundations. First, it will have acknowledged and built upon the work and achievements of the last planning period. Second, it will be rooted in a combination of researched evidence and futures thinking.

Summary

This case study demonstrates both the evolutionary nature of development planning in schools and the incorporation of procedures that will enable significant reengineering to take place. Current practice is very effective at providing checklists for action but the limitations are clear. Typical plans do not provide a means of identifying and working towards a futures perspective. Also, the lack of distinction between intent and operational planning does not enable recognition of the key goals that require thought and maturation before they can be translated into planning objectives. The new model enables this distinction and provides a continuum of thought and action.

Schools are pitched at different places in a hierarchy that has three discernible levels:

- Schools where development planning is still about making lists for action as a management tool for bringing about change. *Longsands was in this position up to three years ago.*
- Schools where development planning is beginning to recognise the need for a futures perspective. *Longsands is now at this stage.*
- Schools that are now ready and able to benefit from the full application of the new model. *Longsands will be ready for this when it produces its next plan in two years time.*

Experience suggests that schools evolve through these levels at different rates and in different ways. This case study exemplifies how the new thinking can be applied to the work of schools and adapted accordingly to meet their particular need. A fundamental thread running through the case study is the need for schools to gradually embrace the concepts of futures thinking. Steadily, and with growing confidence, they must undertake the necessary and often radical reengineering required to meet the needs of students as they grow up into a world which is very different to the one we live in now.

Appendix
Philadelphia – strategic intent at the system wide level

The following is a letter from David Hornbeck, Superintendent of Schools in Philadelphia, setting out the 'Children Achieving Action Design'. It is followed by the Action Design itself which shows how a series of intents with capability-building measures are attempting to 'leverage up' the performance of the school system in Philadelphia. We are grateful to David and to Vicky Phillips, Executive Director of Children Achieving, for sharing this approach with us. We believe that it is an outstanding example of how strategic intent can be used to build capability within the education system in order to achieve significantly higher performance levels of student learning.

To the Board of Education and the Citizens of Philadelphia:

I came to Philadelphia 176 days ago for one reason: to be part of becoming the first major American city where virtually all its public school children perform at high levels.

Today I present to the Philadelphia Board of Education the Action Design to meet this goal. Development of this Action Design is built on the aggressive leadership and vision of the Board, which had been so clearly committed to school reform before I came, and to Children Achieving since. Embodying the contributions of many friends of our children, this plan translates into practice the Children Achieving agenda. It charts our course for the next four and one half years and, indeed, its accomplishments will lead us into the 21st century confident of the future. Its comprehensive scope ranges from new high standards our students must meet to compete in our global economy, to the additional time our teachers will need to prepare both themselves and the students, and to the reorganization of the entire School District to full-day kindergarten.

The plan follows the ten components of Children Achieving. Within each component, an introduction provides a vision and rationale; specific strategies describe how to proceed toward this vision; and a timeline identifies significant features of our schedule.

Acknowledging all the difficult decisions and hard work leading to this Action Design, it still remains the easy part because it simply describes the conditions needed for *Children Achieving*. The District cannot create these conditions alone. Success will require the commitment of us all.

Many partnerships have already begun. Hundreds of friends of Philadelphia's children have participated in Task Forces and Consultative Committees. Their hard work and recommendations formed the foundation for this design. It also reflects input I received from over 1,000 administrators, teachers and parents from all of our schools. Another invaluable contribution came from 22 community meetings across the city, organized by the Alliance for Public School Advocates.

All these groups have expressed interest in continuing their involvement. I look forward to continuing to work with them. My warm personal thanks go to all these participants, and especially to the individuals who led this prodigious effort: Ms Shelly Yanoff, Task Forces Co-ordinator; Ms Rochelle Nichols-Soloman and Ms Jane Malone, the Alliance; Mr Richard Mandel, Director of the Philadelphia Public/Business Partnership for Reform, and Professor Ralph Smith from the Annie E. Casey Foundation.

Children Achieving will produce immeasurable rewards for us all. But it also places extraordinary demands upon all:

- Our children can count on having safe classrooms in which they find stimulating, relevant and supportive instruction. In return, they must become active learners, attend school regularly and behave in ways that support the learning of others.
- School staff can count on increased resources, support for their personal professional growth and increased autonomy. In return, school staff must accept increased accountability for improved student achievement.
- Parents can count on safer, more intimate academic environments and a strong voice in designing their children's programs. In return, they must be willing to support their own child's daily readiness and respect for school and to advocate for education.
- Business can count on graduates who are prepared to fill

their jobs. In return, they need to support *Children Achieving* and make these jobs available.

- Taxpayers and elected representatives can count on an efficient use of resources to prepare graduates to contribute to our society. In return, they must provide the necessary resources and support.

Can Philadelphia be the first major American city to succeed in having its children achieve? The answer is a resounding yes! High expectations are precisely the first step of *Children Achieving* and of its Action Design. If each of us believes that virtually all children can learn at high levels and acts on that belief, children will achieve. If we don't, our children will fall behind the rest of the world. Timid, little steps won't do it. Changes at the margins only delay a continuing decline. We must all do our part for bold, comprehensive reform.

The time is now. The place is Philadelphia.

David Hornbeck
Superintendent, 6 February 1995

Children Achieving Action Design

No city with any significant number and diversity of students has ever succeeded in having a large proportion of its young people achieve at high levels. But for school reform to succeed, it must succeed in our great cities. The Action Design is organized around the ten components of the *Children Achieving* agenda.

I   Set high expectations for everyone

The operating assumption for all policies, planning and decisions will be that all students – including those from low-income families, racial and language minorities, students with disabilities, and other populations we have historically failed – can and will achieve at high levels.

This proposition will be the standard against which we measure policy and behavior. Schools will use it in designing curriculum, assigning students and selecting professional development. The system will use it in setting standards, designing incentive systems and allocating resources.

This standard – that all children can and will achieve at high levels – will create a school system committed to continuous improvement, in which we return again and again to seek new answers to the questions *how* do we teach, *who* teaches, *where* does learning take place, and *when* does learning occur? It will force us to ask the hard questions and implement the non-traditional answers.

We will know that we are on the way to success as more and more children move toward meeting high standards. We will know that we have gotten it right when every child is successful. Specific strategies include:

- Establish one set of rigorous, challenging graduation standards with appropriate benchmarks at the fourth and eighth grades.
- Develop opportunity-to-learn standards to: ensure that all students are given adequate opportunities to meet the new standards; enable students, parents and the community to hold schools accountable for results; and enable teachers, administrators and schools to hold the system and community accountable.
- Develop a school culture that is flexible and innovative.
- Create an Office of Equality Assurance to make sure that all schools have adequate resources and engage in the type of practices needed for all children to achieve at high levels.

2 Design accurate performance indicators to hold everyone accountable for results

Trying hard is not good enough, either for those who work in the system or, ultimately, for students. Performance is what counts, and the District will use better ways of measuring it. We will implement an assessment system sophisticated enough to tell us whether our students are achieving high standards and whether they are performing well compared to students in other cities and states. We will design an incentive system that offers meaningful rewards for good performance, assistance for students and educators who need it and consequences for poor performance. Specific strategies include:

- Implement a system of performance-based assessments tied to the new high standards for students.
- Design valid assessments for students of diverse language background.
- Design an incentive system for staff that links achievement by all students, including those whom we have historically failed, to real rewards and penalties.
- Establish an Office of Standards, Assessment and Accountability in 1995 to develop standard and assessment strategies and improve the new accountability system.
- Begin negotiating with the city's companies, colleges, universities

and unions to assure that all students who meet the graduation standards are admitted to college or hired for a job.

3 Shrink the centralised bureaucracy and let schools make more decisions

Professionals who are expected to produce results and be judged on those results should have the right to determine how they practise their profession. Thus, significant authority to determine the nature of the school learning environment will move down the bureaucratic pipeline so that those closer to the students make more of the decisions that shape instruction.

The School District of Philadelphia will turn the system on its head in order to create an operating environment that will permit all children to achieve at high levels. Learning communities will become the focal point of the District rather than the bottom rung of a hierarchy. In this new scenario, schools will make the important decisions around teaching and learning, and the central office will set standards, assess progress, monitor for equity, and act as a guide and provider of resources and support. Specific strategies include:

- Organise schools into small learning communities of 200 to 500 students.
- Establish school councils to govern school-wide policies and resources.
- Reorganise schools by feeder pattern into 22 neighborhood clusters of six to ten elementary schools, two to four middle schools and a comprehensive high school.
- Restructure and downsize the central office so that it becomes more responsive and accountable to learning communities, schools and school clusters.
- Allocate decisions about resources to schools in a way that encourages efficiency and innovation and that promotes high achievement by all students in all schools.
- Develop a system of client-centred services and supports.

4 Provide intensive and sustained professional development to all staff

The goal of the professional development system will be to empower every teacher, administrator and staff member to develop the knowledge, skills and behaviors required to create learning settings that enable all students to demonstrate high levels of achievement. Specific strategies include:

- Provide 20 days of time or its budgetary equivalent for the professional development of all school-based teachers, administrators and staff.
- Make professional development resources convenient for teachers and administrators to use.
- Provide specific professional development opportunities, some ongoing, some transitional, that target priority needs.

5 Make sure that all students are ready for schools

Services for Philadelphia's young children are inadequate in quantity, uneven in quality, fragmented, often difficult to access, governed by conflicting rules, regulations and eligibility requirements, and supervised by different offices or bureaucracies. Consequently, children and families are denied the services that are prerequisites to school and lifetime success; schools expend substantial resources addressing problems that could have been prevented; and society pays later in costs associated with unemployment and social disarray.

In addressing this situation, we need not choose between the dictates of our hearts and those of our head – that which is morally imperative is also economically sound. Specific strategies include:

- Provide a developmentally appropriate full-day kindergarten program to all eligible children.
- In partnership with the Department of Health and Human Services, create a Children and Families Authority.

6 Provide students with the community support and services they need to succeed in school

Community services and supports can make the difference between success and failure. Children who are unhealthy, hungry, abused, ill-housed, ill-clothed or otherwise face problems outside the school, will not achieve at high levels. We must dramatically expand the services and supports needed to reduce the impact of these major barriers to learning.

Schools and communities will explore new ways of working together and supporting each other in the vital task of educating the next generation. The District will forge new relationships with organizations in the larger community that can meet students' non-academic needs, link students with necessary services or actually bring the programs into the schools. The School District will do its part, but so must the public and private agencies outside the school. Specific strategies include:

- Link students with health and social services agencies.

- Ensure that each school has an ongoing relationship with at least one community based organization.
- Recruit and match 10,000 new volunteers with schools.
- Conduct a campaign to prevent student pregnancies, and make sure that students who are pregnant or parenting have access to the health and social services they and their children need.

7 Provide up-to-date technology and institutional materials

Technology can fundamentally transform how schools and teachers serve students. It can connect teachers and students to enormously expanded educational resources and individualized instruction, and begin to expand the boundaries of the educational setting beyond the classroom and even beyond the school itself.

Technology can also profoundly improve the administrative processes and procedures that support classroom instruction, helping us with report development, inventory control, scheduling and hosts of other administrative matters. Specific strategies include:

- Provide all schools with the resources and support needed to have one computer for every six students.
- Transform libraries into technology resource centres.
- Consolidate responsibility for the District's technology infrastructure into a single office.
- Conduct a comprehensive analysis and make a five-year recommendation of what technology and information resources will be needed to support student learning.

8 Engage the public in shaping, understanding, supporting and participating in school reform

In order to make the revolutionary changes proposed in the Action Design, we need the public's permission. The schools belong to them – as citizens, as taxpayers and as parents. Community after community across the United States has learned, often when it was too late, that schools will not improve without sustained public understanding and support.

Our challenges are straightforward. Citizens need to understand why changes of this magnitude are needed. They need to believe that school officials are on the right track in carrying out these changes. They must be actively encouraged to take part in our efforts to improve Philadelphia's public schools. They must be given plenty of opportunity to see first-hand the work in progress. And they must have the tools by which to hold educators accountable for results. Specific strategies include:

- Continue listening closely to what the community wants and expects from its schools and its children
- Develop messages and strategies that clearly explain to people what Philadelphia's schools are doing and why.
- Support the Alliance's efforts to mobilize and organize the community in support of high-quality education.
- Build the capacity of all District staff to be better ambassadors for educational excellence.

9 Ensure adequate resources and use them effectively

Adequate resources are a common-sense precondition to virtually all children achieving at high levels. Additional resources are not the only requirement for radical change – they are not even the most important ingredient – but additional resources are an absolute prerequisite for *dramatically improving* student outcomes. The provision of these resources is a key accountability indicator of the extent to which Philadelphians and those in the state capital understand the consequences of a failing Philadelphia School District and support the challenging goal of *Children Achieving*.

The restructuring of District operations and the delivery of services clearly will entail significant recurring costs and non-recurring transition costs. But we also are exploring new ways of making more effective use of existing resources. Specific strategies include:

- Aggressively improve efficiency and effectiveness in non-instructional areas.
- Investigate alternative financing opportunities, such as asset sales, tax lien, sales, debt restructuring, forward float agreements for school district sinking funds, and funding debt.
- Ensure that the District is making the best use of existing space and planning strategically for future space requirements.
- Ensure that the District is drawing on all resources to the maximum extent possible.
- Augment the District's operating budget with ancillary private resources, such as the Annenberg Foundation grant, and funds from other foundations and corporations.
- Aggressively pursue greater equity and adequacy of government resources and their distribution.
- Redesign teaching and learning so that the who, how, where and when are viewed as variables and student achievement remains the constant.

10 Be prepared to address all of these priorities together and for the long-term – starting now

The *Children Achieving* agenda is not a 'pick and choose' menu. We must approach the challenge of education reform in a comprehensive and integrated way. If one or more features of the whole agenda is not implemented, its power to yield high achievement by all students will be significantly diminished.

The *Children Achieving* agenda describes a reality that does not exist now in any city or school district with a diverse population. Philadelphia has no one to emulate – we are on the frontier. We have already begun the hard work of becoming the first major urban school system in which large numbers of students in all schools across the District achieve at high levels. But we have much farther to go.

We ask that the broader community join us in our vision of an educational system where all children can achieve at high levels and help us create a system of:

Learning communities, characterised by:

- children who are learning at high levels and graduates who succeed in work and post-secondary education;
- teachers who guide, coach and prompt students, and feel engaged in a challenging intellectual endeavour in which they make important decisions and accept responsibility;
- technology that expands the classroom walls;
- teaching and assessment strategies that emphasize intellectual accomplishment.

Schools, characterised by:

- high expectations for all students;
- parents who are involved and active at every level;
- an emphasis on high quality, nurturing relationships;
- comprehensive support for the whole child;
- time for teacher collaboration and reflective practice.

Clustered learning communities which:

- foster teaching and learning across the K-12 continuum;
- focus on student transitions: home to school, school to school and school to work and/or higher education;
- leverage services and support through shared resources;
- foster initiatives to accelerate learning for at-risk students;
- co-ordinate supports for families and children.

A Central Office, organised to:

- ensure equity defined as high achievement for *all* students;
- ensure accountability through clearly articulated District-wide standards, backed by rewards, penalties and supports;
- deliver responsive, high quality and efficient services with a customer focus;
- maintain a partnership with collective bargaining organizations for school reform;
- engage in long-range strategic planning that strives for continuous improvement.

This vision is wholly achievable if we, as a community, share the belief that it is both possible and necessary to transform the School District of Philadelphia for the economic and civic future of our children, our city and ultimately our nation.

Contributors

Brent Davies is Professor and Director of the International Educational Leadership Centre at the University of Lincolnshire and Humberside. Brent has designed and led International MBAs at Leeds Metropolitan University and the University of Lincolnshire and Humberside and designed the International taught doctorate in Educational Leadership at the University of Lincolnshire and Humberside. He has established strong international links for developing cross-national work in Educational Leadership. Brent is Chair of the International Committee of the British Educational Management and Administration Society. He has written eleven books (eight with Linda Ellison, including *School Leadership for the 21st Century: A Competency and Knowledge Approach*) and over fifty articles on educational leadership and management, focusing more recently on reengineering and futures thinking in education and new approaches to school planning. Brent has worked extensively with headteachers in the UK and overseas to develop new approaches to school leadership and management.

Linda Ellison is Principal Lecturer in Educational Leadership at the Centre for Leadership in Education and Training at Leeds Metropolitan University. She has designed and led major masters awards and currently has overall responsibility for the leadership and management area. She has written nine books, (eight with Brent Davies including *School Leadership for the 21st Century: A Competency and Knowledge Approach*). She has a number of research projects in the area of school planning and leadership development and has published widely in academic and professional journals. She has worked with school principals in a variety of countries including the UK, Hong Kong, Australia, New Zealand and the USA. Linda is an Assessor with the National Educational Assessment Centre, the Editor of the journal, *Management in Education*, a member of the National Council of BEMAS (The British Educational Management and Administration Society) and of its International Committee.

Case study contributors:

Sue Cowans is an Assistant Headteacher at the Philip Morant School in Colchester, with responsibility for assessment and examinations. She has worked in a variety of schools in London, Cambridge and Essex and her involvement in assessment has grown from experience as a Head of Geography and from work as an Assistant Examiner with the Cambridge Board. Her work in using assessment in setting targets to develop strategies aimed at school improvement stems from research carried out over a period of years, which was written up as part of an M.Sc. at Anglia University.

Robert Gwynne has been a head for twelve years. Before leading Longsands College in Cambridgeshire, he was Principal of the inner city Wycliffe Community College in Leicestershire for six years. Previously he taught science in comprehensive schools in Germany, Peterborough, Cyprus and Yorkshire. He teaches on Masters degree courses specialising in leadership and management. He is completing doctoral studies at the International Educational Leadership Centre at the University of Lincolnshire and Humberside.

David Jones recently retired as head of the Philip Morant School in Colchester. This was his second Headship and he also worked in four schools in Staffordshire and Essex. In 1989 he was seconded to BP International to work with the Management Training and Development Unit. Out of this experience came a programme for the training and development of headteachers based on the best practice of various blue chip companies. In 1996 he completed an MBA in Education Management at Leeds Metropolitan University with a dissertation on 'School Improvement Through a Value Added Approach'.

Howard Kennedy has been a head for fourteen years in 8–12, 5–12, 3–12 and 3–11 age-range schools. He spent a year at Oxford University analysing the role of the headteacher in the decision-making process in schools. He has undertaken an International MBA in Educational Leadership at the International Educational Leadership Centre at the University of Lincolnshire and Humberside. Howard has also managed a semi-professional football club which he felt was an ideal preparation for headship.

References

Abbott, R., Steadman S. and Birchenhough M. (1988) *GRIDS School Handbooks*, 2nd ed., Primary and Secondary versions, York: Longman for the SCDC.

Barber, M. (1996) *The Learning Game*, London: Golancz.

Beare, H. and Slaughter, R. (1993) *Education for the Twenty First Century*, London: Routledge.

Boisot, M. (1995) 'Preparing for turbulence' in B. Garratt (ed.), *Developing Strategic Thought*, London: McGraw-Hill.

Bowman, C. and Asch, D. (1987) *Strategic Management*, Basingstoke: Macmillan.

Broadhead, P., Cuckle, P., Hodgson, J. and Dunford, J. (1996) 'Improving Primary Schools through School Development Planning', *Education Management and Administration* Vol. 24 No. 3: 277–290.

Caldwell, B. J. (1997a) 'The Future of Public Education', *Education Management and Administration* Vol. 25 No. 4: 357–370.

Caldwell, B. J. (1997b) 'Global trends and expectations for the further reform of schools' and 'Thinking in time a gestalt for schools of the new millennium' in B. Davies and L. Ellison *School Leadership for the 21st century: A Competency and Knowledge Approach*, London: Routledge.

Caldwell, B. J. and Hayward, D. K. (1998) *The Future of Schools: Lessons from the Reform of Public Education*, London: Falmer Press.

Caldwell, B. J. and Spinks, J. M. (1992) *Leading the Self-mamaging School*, London: Falmer Press.

Cannon, T. (1996) *Welcome to the Revolution: Managing Paradox in the 21st Century*, London: Pitman.

Carr, D. K. and Johansson, H. J., (1995) *Best Practice Reengineering*, New York: McGraw-Hill.

Davies, B. (1997) 'Rethinking the educational context: a reengineering approach' in B. Davies and L. Ellison *School Leadership for the 21st Century: A Competency and Knowledge Approach*, London: Routledge.

Davies, B. and Ellison, L. (1992) *School Development Planning*, Harlow: Longman.

Davies, B. and Ellison, L. (1993) 'Parental Choice and School Response' paper presented at the British Educational Management and Administration Society, National Research Conference, Sheffield, February.

Davies, B. and Ellison, L (1997a) *School Leadership for the 21st Century: A Competency and Knowledge Approach*, London: Routledge.

Davies, B. and Ellison, L (1997b) 'Futures and strategic perspectives in school planning' Paper presented at the American Educational Research Association Annual Meeting, Chicago, March.

Davies, B. and Ellison, L (1997c) *Strategic Marketing for Schools*, London: Pitman.

Davies, B. and West-Burnham, J. (1997) *Reengineering and Total Quality in Schools*, London: Pitman.

Dent, H. S. (1995) *Jobshock*, New York: St Martin's Press.

DES (1989) *Planning for School Development: Advice for Governors, Headteachers and Teachers*, London: HMSO.

DES (1991) *Development Planning: A Practical Guide*, London: DES.

Dettman, P. (1997) 'The laptop revolution' in B. Davies and J. West-Burnham (eds), *Reengineering and Total Quality in Schools*, London: Pitman.

DFEE (1996) *Setting Targets to Raise Standards: A Survey of Good Practice*, London: DFEE.

DFEE (1997a) *Excellence in Schools*, London: HMSO.

DFEE (1997b) *From Targets to Action*, London: DFEE.

Drucker, P. (1993) *Post-capitalist Society*, New York: Harper Business.

Ellison, L. and Davies, B. (1990) 'Planning in education management' in B. Davies, L. Ellison, A. Osborne and J. West-Burnham (eds), *Education Management for the 1990s*, Harlow: Longman.

Fullan, M. (1993) *Change Forces*, London: Falmer Press.

Gates, B. (1995) *The Road Ahead*, New York: Penguin.

Gerstner, L. V., Semerad, R. D., Doyle, D. P. and Johnson, W. B. (1994) *Reinventing Education: America's Public Schools*, New York: Dutton.

Giles, C. (1997) *School Development Planning: A Practical Guide to the Strategic Management Process*, Plymouth: Northcote House.

Glatter, R., Woods, P. and Bagley, C. (1995) *Diversity, Differentiation and Hierarchy: School Choice and Parental Preferences*, ESRC/CEPAM Invitation Seminar, Milton Keynes, 7–8 June.

Guardian (1997) 'Three into five won't go' *Guardian Education* 24/6/97 Schools 3.

Hamel, G. and Prahalad, C. K. (1989) 'Strategic Intent', *Harvard Business Review*, May/June.

Hammer, M. and Champy, J. (1993) *Reengineering the Corporation*, New York: HarperCollins.

Hammer, M. and Stanton, S. A. (1995) *The Reengineering Revolution: A Handbook*, New York: Harper Business.

Handy, C. (1994) *The Empty Raincoat: Making Sense of the Future*, London: Hutchinson.

Hargreaves, D. (1994) *The Mosaic of Learning: Schools and Teachers for the New Century*, London: Demos.

Hargreaves, D. (1997) 'A Road to the Learning Society' *School Leadership & Management* Vol. 17 No. 1: 9–21.

Hargreaves, D. and Hopkins, D. (1991) *The Empowered School: The Management and Practice of Development Planning*, London: Cassell.

Johnson, G. and Scholes, K. (1993) *Exploring Corporate Strategy*, 3rd edn, Hemel Hempstead: Prentice Hall.

Johnson, G. and Scholes, K. (1997) *Exploring Corporate Strategy*, 4th edn, London: Prentice Hall.

Kawasaki, G. (1995) *How to Drive Your Competition Crazy*, New York: Hyperion.

Lewis, J. (1997) 'From a blank sheet of paper' in B. Davies and J. West-Burnham (eds), *Reengineering and Total Quality in Schools*, London: Pitman.

MacGilchrist, B., Mortimore, P., Savage, J. and Beresford, C., (1995) *Planning Matters: The Impact of Development Planning in Primary Schools*, London: Paul Chapman Publishing.

Mintzberg, H. (1994) *The Rise and Fall of Strategic Planning*, Hemel Hempstead: Prentice Hall.

Mintzberg, H., Ghoshal, S. and Quinn, J .B. (1995) *The Strategy Process* (Euro. edn) Hemel Hempstead: Prentice Hall.

National Audit Office (1994) *Value for Money at Grant-maintained Schools: A Review of Performance*, London: HMSO.

Office for Standards in Education (1994) *Improving Schools*, London: HMSO.

Ohmae, K. (1995) *The End of the Nation State: The Rise of Regional Economies*, London: HarperCollins.

Pollard, W. (1997) 'The leader who serves' in F. Hesselbein and R. Beckhard (eds), *The Leader of the Future*, San Francisco: Jossey Bass.

Porter, M. (1987) 'Corporate Strategy: The State of Strategic Thinking', *The Economist* 23 May.

Porter, M. (1980) *Competitive Strategy*, New York: Free Press.

Porter, P. (1993) *Awaken the Genius*, Phoenix, Ariz.: Purelight Publishing.

Puffitt, R., Stoten, B. and Winkley, D. (1992) *Business Planning for Schools*, Harlow: Longman.

Purkey, W. W. and Novak, J. M. (1996) *Inviting School Success*, Belmont Calif.: Wadsworth Publishing Co.

Reich, R. (1992) *The Work of Nations*, New York: Vintage Books.

Senge, P. (1990) *The Fifth Discipline*, New York: Doubleday.

Sergiovanni, T. (1992) *Moral Leadership*, San Francisco: Jossey Bass.

Skelton, M., Reeves, G. and Playfoot, D. (1991) *Development Planning for Primary Schools*, Windsor: NFER.

Southorn, N. (1997) 'Reengineering post-16 courses' in B. Davies and J. West-Burnham (eds), *Reengineering and Total Quality in Schools*, London: Pitman.

Stoll, L. and Fink, D. (1996) *Changing our Schools*, Buckingham: Open University Press.

Taberrer, R. (1997) Lecture given to the Yorkshire and Humberside Region of BEMAS, Sheffield, 25 June.

Times Educational Supplement 2 (1997) 'Prehistoric Pretensions' 28.02.97.

Walden, G. (1996) *We Should Know Better: Solving the Education Problem*, London: Fourth Estate.

West, A. (1992) 'Factors Affecting Choice of School for Middle Class Parents: Implications for Marketing', *Educational Management and Administration*, Vol. 20 No. 4: 223–230.

West, M. and Ainscow, M. (1991) *Managing School Development: A Practical Guide*, London: Fulton.

West-Burnham, J. (1997) *Managing Quality in Schools*, London: Pitman.

Index